The Writer in the Landscape

SCRIPTA HUMANISTICA®

Directed by
BRUNO M. DAMIANI
The Catholic University of America

THE WRITER IN THE LANDSCAPE :

Authorial Self-Representation
and
Literary Form in the Landscape Writings of
Unamuno and *Azorín*

by

Mary Ruth Strzeszewski

SCRIPTA HUMANISTICA®
157

Publisher and Distributor

SCRIPTA HUMANISTICA®

1383 Kersey Lane

Potomac, Maryland 20854 USA

Tel. (301) 294 - 7949

Fax. (301) 424 - 9584

Internet : www.scriptahumanistica.com

E-mail : info@scriptahumanistica.com

S.H. # 157

I.S.B.N. 1-882528-47-6

Price : $ 69.95

Printed in the United States of America

2006

Contents

Acknowledgments

My thanks are owed to many more people than I can include in this list, among these: to Professor Gonzalo Sobejano, for his extraordinary guidance as my dissertation advisor, and to all other members of my dissertation committee—Professors Alfred MacAdam, Gustavo Pérez Firmat, Mirella Servodidio, and Xavier Vila—for their very helpful feedback; to Professor Patricia Grieve, for her guidance and supportiveness throughout my graduate studies; to Addette L. Williams, Ph.D., for seeing this project and its author all the way through; here at The City College of New York (CUNY), to Dean James Watts and Professor Juan Carlos Mercado for creating the conditions for me to bring this project to completion, and to all of my colleagues who I am so privileged to work with for their continued support and mentorship; to the Program for Cultural Cooperation and the PSC-CUNY Research Foundation for their generous research support; and to the Biblioteca Nacional de España and to the Casa-Museo Unamuno for their assistance with the research. To the each of the following people I owe a very special, heartfelt debt of gratitude: Elizabeth Amann, Astrid Benedek, Chela Bodden, Tina Jacobson, David Lazar, Richie Narvaez, and Adam Zimmerman. Finally, my sincere thanks to Professor Bruno Damiani and Scripta Humanistica for publishing my manuscript.

Introduction

The emergence of the Spanish landscape at the turn of the century as an important subject, both in literature and in painting, was influenced by a variety of factors. Two of the most important texts in stimulating interest in the Spanish landscape—the desire to "buscar a España en su cuerpo" (Franco 296)—were Miguel de Unamuno's *En torno al casticismo* (1895) and Ángel Ganivet's *Idearium español* (1897). Both authors purport to "find fundamental and persistent national traits through an examination of fundamental and persistent physical conditions" (Ramsden 22). Ganivet emphasizes the importance of Spain's peninsular geography in the development of Spanish character and its relations with the rest of the world. Unamuno advocates the idea that knowledge of Spain must come from a study of its *intrahistoria* embodied in the people and physical environment of its *pueblos*, those:

> ordinary men and women, people without history who day by day go about their ordinary work. It is these people who are the real bond between historic moments, who are the all-important, unbroken, unconscious, intra-historic element, the bearers of the true, eternal tradition [. . .]. (Ramsden 18)

For both authors, as Ramsden points out, "the probing of national character is no mere academic exercise. It has profound practical consequences. In the recognition and revitalizing of the fundamental national spirit lies the way out of Spain's psychological dilemma of lost directions" (28).

Several institutional developments contributed to the exploration and representation of the Spanish landscape. Giner de los Ríos together with other krausists founded the Institución Libre de Enseñanza in 1876, for the purpose of fostering "aquellas cualidades que desearían ver arraigadas en el conjunto de la sociedad—tolerancia, laicismo, espíritu democrático y talante científico" (Fox 32). A central part of the curriculum was excursions to all parts of Spain to promote students' knowledge of their country through direct experience. The Institución, interested in promoting positive science, supported geographical research. Geography was one of the most recent sciences, having been recognized "en el ambiente positivista entre 1850 y 1900, nacida en el primer momento como un método esencialmente descriptivo que atendía a los aspectos físicos del territorio," but which later, under the influence of Humbolt, was extended into the fields of history and aesthetics (Pena 75).

Another important development that affected literary representation of landscape came in the field of the plastic arts, with the establishment of the Cátedra de Paisaje in the Academia Nacional de Bellas Artes in 1844. With the creation of this position, landscape painting was officially recognized as a significant genre. Prior to this time, examples of Spanish landscape painting were sparse, although with notable exceptions:

> Los fondos de paisaje medievales adquirieron gran belleza en Berruguete, por ejemplo; de forma excepcional y original pintó a Toledo El Greco; durante los siglos XVII y XVIII los aires europeos se percibieron en nuestra pintura en escasa medida [. . .].

> Velázquez habría de aportar sus paisajes de la Villa Medicis, Mazo pintó vistas de ciudades, y B. Aguero conoció y estudió para sus temas los loreneses de las colecciones reales [. . .]. (Pena 25)

In the second half of the nineteenth century, painters in search of a Spanish tradition took a new interest the Castilian landscape in the background of paintings by El Greco and Velázquez. With Carlos de Haes's assumption of the Cátedra de Paisaje, techniques of French realist painting were disseminated and the genre flourished. The connection between developments in painting and descriptive writing in the Generation of '98 was particularly strong. Pena observes the influence of landscape painting in writings of Azorín in particular, and Gayana Jurkevich has extensively analyzed the relationship between Azorín's writing and the visual arts.

Miguel de Unamuno (1864-1936) and José Martínez Ruiz [Azorín] (1873-1967) were two of the writers of this period who most extensively incorporated the Spanish landscape into their work. In their short writings on landscape, Spain's *fin-de-siecle* fascination with its newly rediscovered national space reaches its maximum expression in prose. While distinct in many respects, Unamuno and Azorín are responsible, more than any other writers of their period, for taking landscape beyond the boundaries of the novel and establishing it as a prose subject in its own right, in *sui generis* short writings innovated from the flexible form of the literary article.

Azorín and Unamuno both wrote in virtually every genre. Azorín was a novelist, essayist, and playwright. Unamuno more than once declared his desire to be regarded as principally a poet, yet his career and his stature as a writer were based primarily on his essays, fiction, and plays. Azorín, on the other hand, declares in his *Memorias inmemoriales* that he "never thought of himself as a writer, but rather as a painter" (Jurkevich, *A Poetics of Time and Space*, 284). Ángel del Río observes that Unamuno, who practiced virtually every major genre, was able to "ensanchar los límites clásicos del ensayo hasta las fronteras de otros géneros: novela, cuento, o poesía" (78). Although Ortega falls outside the scope of this work, it is impossible not to mention him as he also extensively practiced the descriptive essay. In his article "Ortega narrador," Gonzalo Sobejano notes that Ortega never completely identified with any one form of expression. His vocation, says Sobejano, "era el pensamiento, el afán de claridad sobre las cosas" (*Ortega* 184). Azorín and Unamuno share Ortega's lack of definitive identification with any one genre. Their extensive cultivation of landscape descriptions may be seen as an attempt to find a vehicle for creative impulses that could not be fully exercised within the novel. It seems safe to say that landscape, as a subject for prose writing, was legitimized within the novel and the essay at the turn of the century, but that writers such as Unamuno and Azorín found that the aesthetic and philosophic potential of description exceeded the bounds that these genres set upon it (as subordinate to idea on the one hand and plot and character on the other), and cultivated other more open forms of prose.

While description has conventionally played a subordinate role in fiction, the represented world of a narrative became more detailed through the development of realism. Detailed and evocative descriptions of urban landscapes are abundant in nineteenth-century realist novels. In *Peñas Arriba* the natural landscape is central to the novel. The role of landscape in the novel reached a new intensity with publication of Azorín's *La voluntad* and Pío Baroja's *Camino de perfección* in 1902. While both works were received with critical enthusiasm, the ambivalent response of some readers towards the importance given to description in *Camino de perfección* is telling. While Azorín intends to praise Baroja's novel when he calls it "una colección magnífica de paisajes," other readers will consider this a motive for criticism. Weston and Noma Flint point out that:

> the few interpretations of *Camino de perfección (Pasión mística)* which appeared between its publication in 1902 and the late 1960s have reflected the apparent amorphousness of the book. As the plot seems to develop, it dissolves into a series of disconnected tableaux and descriptions of landscape, which are no longer a background but assume primary importance—indeed, some critics claim that they usurp the place of the protagonist. (9)

The perplexity aroused by *Camino de perfección* reflects the notion that landscape, or description in general, should be subordinate to other values in a novel, particularly plot and character. It is this attitude that Azorín rejects openly in *La voluntad*, when Yuste says that "Lo que da la medida de un artista es su sentimiento de la naturaleza, del paisaje [. . .]" (130).

Unamuno echoes this sentiment in his preface to the 1920 edition of *Andanzas y visiones españolas*, in which he outlines his attitude towards description in his own novelistic production.

> El que siguiendo mi producción literaria se haya fijado en mis novelas, excepción hecha de la primera de ellas en tiempo, de *Paz en la guerra*, habrá podido observar que rehuyo en ellas las descripciones y hasta el situarlas en época y lugar determinados, en darles color temporal y local. . . . Y ello obedece al propósito de dar a mis novelas la mayor intensidad y el mayor carácter dramáticos posibles, reduciéndolas, en cuanto quepa, a diálogos y relato de acción y de sentimientos [. . .]. (522)

He concludes that the reader who enjoys landscape descriptions will look for them for their own sake, and it is in response to that demand he says that he offers the present collection. In addition to affirming the attitude that excessive description can detract from narrative, Unamuno justifies "landscapes for their own sake" by stating that there is already a readership for such writings.

Unamuno and Azorín were both influenced by travel writing, and both lamented the literary deformation of the Spanish landscape by various foreign writers in the past. Travel is also presented in marked contrast to tourism. Both Unamuno and Azorín speak disparagingly of the developing tourist industry. En "Ciudad, campos, paisajes y recuerdos," Unamuno writes: "¿Hay algo más azarante, más molesto, más prosaico que el turista? El enemigo de quien viaja por pasión, por alegría o por tristeza, para recordar o para olvidar, es el que viaja por vanidad o por moda, es ese horrible e insoportable turista" (546-547). In contrast to the overstimulated adventure seeker and the jaded tourist, the traveler in the writings of Unamumo and Azorín is a contemplative one, a traveler in need, seeking contact and stimulation but also consolation.

Movement is essential in the landscape writings of Azorín and Unamuno. Many of these writings feature departures, usually from the city, with its accompanying sense of transition and distance, as well as arrivals, colored by feelings of fatigue and anticipation. What is clear is that the experience of landscape requires movement, both literal and metaphorical: a shift from one's ordinary perspective. The paradox of landscape is that, while it is allegedly part of the "eternal Spain," its experience is necessarily time-bound and fleeting. Landscape is an interlude in the course of daily life, achieved with effort, sustainable only for short periods of time.

As travel writers, Azorín and Unamuno have a special relationship of intimacy and trust with the reader. The reader of a travel account is invited to participate in the writer's experience almost as a friend. The reader, in fact, is part of the justification for the writing. Also, the reader implicitly trusts the writer to describe only authentic experience: to have actually been where he says he was, to have seen what he says he saw and felt what he says he felt. This is the opposite of the travel writer Unamuno describes in "De vuelta de la cumbre": "Sé de un cronista a quien no le interesan ni los paisajes ni los monumentos arquitectónicos; llega a una ciudad, compra una colección de vistas de ella, se encierra en el hotel, donde se cuida, ante todo, del menú, y se pone, con una guía al lado, a escribir su viaje" (535). While Unamuno recognizes the vital importance of the author's imagination in travel writings, he is clear that his vision must be generated from real contact with a place.

The intimacy between reader and writer is deepened by the writer's solitary condition; even when accompanied by a friend or two, the writer seems to write from an inner solitude. When there is not an explicit first-person narrator, as in some chapters of *Los pueblos*, the emotional register of the writing conveys his presence. The publication of these writings in newspapers and periodicals, which implies the relatively short time between their writing and publication, narrows the temporal distance between writing and reading as well. This intimacy between writer and reader is one of the defining characteristics of Unamuno and Azorín's landscape writings.

But who is the narrator of these writings? The scarceness of biographical references in these writings indicates a distance between the author and the writing, or perceiving self. The "I" of these pieces is a less individualized, more universal self. It is a self that is similar to the one described by Rilke in the following passage from *Letters to a Young Poet*:

> Only the individual who is solitary is like a thing placed under profound laws, and when he goes out in the morning that is just beginning, or looks out into the evening which is full of happening, and if he feels what is going on there, then all status drops from him as from a dead man, though he stands in the midst of sheer life. (47)

Related to the traveler is the pilgrim. The resemblance of the excursions of the *noventayochistas* to pilgrimages is clear and sometimes explicitly thematized in their writings. Sanctified by the ideas of Unamuno and the *institucionistas*, the most remote corner of Spain offers the chance for contact with the profound and invisible forces of the nation's intrahistoria. Landscape descriptions have a didactic quality; in so far as they transmit the writer's experience of these places, they convey knowledge. But they are didactic not only in their content but also in their form; they offer the reader a model of experiencing the existence of the world and his own being.

As has already been mentioned, the evolution of landscape as a literary subject is also closely related to developments in painting. The history of landscape painting in Spain from the mid-nineteenth century is the history of a subject's transition from margin to center. The emergence of Castilian landscape in general underwent a similar transition. Spanish landscape artists began to re-examine the Castilian landscapes in the background of paintings by El Greco and Velázquez. Dolores Franco observes:

> Castilla había estado siempre ahí, con sus llanuras inmensas, con su monotonía de trigales, con sus lomas moteadas de oscuras encinas, con su cielo tersamente azul; y, sin embargo, nunca se le había encontrado bella; nunca se había cantado sino las brumas de las rías gallegas, el verdor de la Montaña, los tonos fuertes de Levante o la gracia armónica de Andalucía. (296)

Ramsden notes that before 1898, Unamuno disliked the Castilian landscape. The "discovery" of Castile implied that the region had always had a latent beauty, but that it took a new way of seeing for that beauty to be experienced. The refocusing of attention from center to margin is a principal theme of the Generation of 1898: the shift from city to town, from hero to intrahistoric men and women, from verdant landscape to the "difficult" beauty of Castile. Azorín writes:

> Lo que necesitamos—nos dice Rilke—son esos paisajes que nuestros padres atravesaban con impaciencia y hastío en sus berlinas cerradas. donde ellos abrían los ojos para bostezar, nosotros abrimos los ojos para ver, vivimos bajo el signo del llano, dos palabras que articulan una sola realidad: la llanura. (Pena 111)

This shift of attention from the center to the margin as a source of meaning presented a challenge to all the representational arts, for its was up to them to make us experience presence where we experience absence, or even less than absence, blankness. It is in this context that I am particularly interested in the landscape descriptions of Unamuno and Azorín. As preeminently prose writers, they are faced with the technical challenge of bringing description, which has traditionally been subordinated to other values, to the fore.

My comparative study begins with their early novels, in which landscape plays a principal role, and goes on to focus on their innovative cultivation of the journal article. From among these articles I have chosen to focus on those in which the author includes himself, or rather, a literary version of himself, as an actor within the text. That is, those articles in which the author not only enunciates, but also performs. Through this study I hope to contribute to the creation of a more coherent critical framework for the appreciation of their use of this new and largely uncodified literary form, the journalistic article as a vehicle for their writings on landscape, as well as to illuminate the relationship between the authors' literary personae in these writings and the changing identity of the writer-intellectual in turn-of-the-century Spain. As Fox has studied, the word "intelectual" as a noun entered Spanish culture around 1898 (Fox, *Ideología* 18). Unamuno and Azorín were intellectuals and artists, and their self-representation in their writings reflects their evolving self-creation as authors.

Chapter 1 of this study focuses on the construction and role of the landscape in Unamuno and Azorín's first major writings on landscape, within the novel, in Unamuno's *Paz en la guerra* and Martínez Ruiz's novels *La voluntad* and *Antonio Azorín.* In this chapter I trace each author's working out of a personal conception of landscape in dialogue with earlier visions of nature such as those associated with Romanticism and the regional novel. Chapter 2 describes each author's construction of a prehistory of the adult intellectual-artist in Unamuno's *Recuerdos de niñez y de mocedad* and Martínez Ruiz's *Las confesiones de un pequeño filósofo,* and the influence of landscape upon the future writer. Chapter 3 is a study of the dimension of "orphanhood" in each author's self-representation, within a context of some nineteenth-century Spanish orphan narratives. The final chapter is devoted to Unamuno and Azorín's travel articles. In it I attempt to describe the characteristics of these unique and innovative writings in relation to existing literary genres and to each author's aesthetic and personal objectives. I consider how Azorín, especially in *Los pueblos*, combines elements of the prose poem, a form that has its modern beginnings in French literature, with elements of the more autochthonous *cuadro de costumbres*, and in doing so at once "nationalizes" this imported form and aesthetically modernizes the space of provincial Spain through the application of a modern, originally urban optic to marginal spaces that were previously the province of regional novels and foreign travel accounts. With respect to Unamuno's travel writings, I study how deterministic ideas cede to an increasingly religious interpretation of landscape. This quality makes Unamuno's vision of landscape basically incompatible with the form of the novel, and may provide another explanation for the author's decision to withdraw landscape descriptions from his novels after *Paz en la guerra* until *San Manuel Bueno, mártir*.

Chapter One

Landscape and the Intellectual in the Early Novels of Unamuno and J. Martínez Ruiz: From Margin to Center

Novel Landscapes: *Paz en la guerra*, *La voluntad* and *Antonio Azorín*

Unamuno's *Paz en la guerra* (1897) and Martínez Ruiz's *La voluntad* (1902) are the first major novels of each writer's career, and in both the landscape plays an important role. Each is set primarily in its author's native region, with interludes in Madrid and other, secondary settings. Laín Entralgo was among the first to point out the importance of the fact that almost all the writers and artists associated with the Generation of '98 were immigrants to the capital:

> Salvo Benavente, madrileño de nación y de vida, todos los del 98 ven la primera luz en la franja más excéntrica de nuestro suelo. Unamuno, Baroja, Maeztu, Bueno y Zuloaga son vascos; Ganivet, granadino; los Machado, sevillanos; *Azorín*, levantino; Valle-Inclán y Menéndez Pidal, gallegos. Los cantores del paisaje castellano son auténticos *descubridores* de Castilla, y acaso por eso pueden ser *inventores* de una Castilla. (30)

Furthermore, each novel was composed during a period when the author was engaged with forms of progressive social thought. Carlos Blanco Aguinaga has described the Generation of '98 as the first intellectuals of the highest rank who tried to cross over to the enemy, fluctuating between anarchism and socialism (38). Although the respective publication dates roughly correspond to the waning of the authors' most radical attitudes, their engagement with progressive ideas informs these works.[1] In this section I will consider the way in which each writer's representation of landscape in his first novel is informed by his ideological attitudes and also by his concern with his relationship to society as an intellectual and writer. To this end, I will focus on each novel's representation of landscape and rural society, and the intellectual character's relationship to these.

My third concern in this section is that of novelistic form. *Paz en la guerra* and *La voluntad* share elements of two novelistic traditions: the *novela de costumbres* and the closely related regional novel. While both *Paz en la guerra* and *La voluntad* are often studied in terms of their digression from realist conventions, their relationship to these other genres is also revealing of their aesthetic intentions. While both authors largely rejected the conservative premises that frequently underlie both the novel of customs and the regional novel, they share with these several key elements: a reaction against prevailing literary modes, the theme of city versus country, extensive descriptive passages of rural scenes, and a structure whose units resemble *cuadros costumbristas*.

---

[1] Blanco Aguinaga sees the Generation of '98 writers' mature preoccupation with landscape as a part of their disengagement with social reform: "[El] paisajismo tiende a ser, con mayor o menor ambigüedad, un rechazo de signo reaccionario" (322). On the whole, he contends, this generation of writers entered "en la realidad histórica por la Historia en tanto que por la vía del paisajismo *sale* de esa realidad" (322).

At the moments in which they wrote their first novels, it would seem that the city is not novelizable material for either Unamuno or Azorín. It is telling that while some of Martínez Ruiz's early short stories are located in urban settings, and *Diario de un enfermo*, which Inman Fox considers a pre-text of *La voluntad*, is principally set in Madrid, *La voluntad* begins and ends in the Levantine areas—Monóvar and Yecla—of Azorín's youth. The urban frame does not appear to have been adequate to Martínez Ruiz for his first fully realized novel, even though part if not all of the writing was carried out in Madrid.[2]

In order to illustrate the relations of Unamuno and Azorín's first novels to these two novelistic genres, I will discuss two novels written by authors whose first literary vocation was that of *costumbrista* writers: Fernán Caballero's *La gaviota* [1849] and José María de Pereda's *Peñas arriba* [1891]. While Pereda's novel is more a regional novel than a novel of customs, it nonetheless has numerous scenes that could be considered *cuadros de costumbres*. Various structural elements of *La gaviota* are shared by *La voluntad*. *Peñas arriba*, in turn, provides a paradigm to which both Unamuno's *Paz en la guerra* and Martínez Ruiz's *Antonio Azorín* may be compared. Since the focus of my study is the representation of landscape, literary form and authorial self-representation, my discussion of the novels will focus on these elements.

La gaviota is generally considered to be the first Spanish novel of customs. Before writing this novel, the author was already highly practiced in the *cuadro de costumbres*. This literary form, fostered by the journalistic press, gained its greatest popularity in the 1830s and 40s, under the practice of Mesonero Romanos and Larra among others. It was dedicated to

---

[2] "Parte de este libro fué compuesta en una casa de la madrileña calle de Relatores [. . .] alternando con el trabajo periodístico" (Martínez Cachero 75).

showing customs, types, and ways of life, both urban and rural, that were felt to be expressive of both national and regional character, particularly those that were perceived to be in danger of disappearing in the wake of industrialization and urbanization. As a dedicated *costumbrista*, Cecilia Böhl von Faber was already very practiced in writing from direct observation. It is this practice and its consequences for Böhl's aesthetics that make her almost, though not quite, a realist. While Böhl's descriptions of landscape are more straightforwardly descriptive, and less emotionally charged than those of Romantic writers such as Bécquer or Gil y Carrasco,[3] her selection of subject matter reveals the author's ideology: "Es pintora de realidades, pero le conviene más el agregado de retratista de vivencias reales, pintorescas" (Caseda Teresa 73). Lily Litvak has described the conservative ideology that can be perceived in her selection and arrangement of landscape elements. The vistas Caballero describes are characterized by:

> variedad y abundancia [. . .] pero la enumeración conforma a un conjunto integrado donde todos los términos están aunados por la estructura, la atmósfera, y sobre todo por un principio de orden y jerarquía [. . .] Abarcando y dominando el paisaje, la cruz corona y ratifica el orden social con el designio divino. (1991, 90)

Böhl's novelistic form is also influenced by *costumbrismo*, as Kirkpatrick has studied:

> *Costumbrismo* emerges as the predominant formal model for narrative construction: with few exceptions the chapters' structure reflects the generic codes of the *cuadro de costumbres* and

[3] Anthony Clarke asserts that there is nothing new in Gil's sense of nature. He synthesizes characteristic traits of landscape description of previous centuries; however, he uses some of these techniques in an original way, and his descriptive passages are atypically lengthy (24).

> associated forms such as the folktale and the short story. Several chapters follow the shorter genres so closely that they form individual set pieces that actively work against any novelistic flow of time or action. Forward movement of the plot is disrupted by the interpolation of a folktale, the story of Mediopollito (ch. 9, pt. 1), and by an account of the notable buildings of Seville. (335)

Readers familiar with Martínez Ruiz's first novel will recognize compositional similarities with *La voluntad*, from its detailed description of the new church of Yecla at the novel's opening, to the extensive landscape descriptions and the inclusion of the parable of the three friends in part 1, chapter 6. The generic heterogeneity that Kirkpatrick observes in *La gaviota* is more pronounced in *Antonio Azorín* and *Las confesiones de un pequeño filósofo*.

Kirkpatrick relates the temporal organization of *La gaviota* to the author's incorporation of discrete cuadros:

> Because the author conceived the main narrative units as tableaux or episodes—static moments whose sequence forms a plot line—time as *durée*, the continuum of experience that links these moments, is excluded from the narration itself and relegated to the silent spaces between the chapters. Some chapters begin with disconcerting jump cuts that abruptly present the reader with new actions or situations whose relation to what precedes is uncertain. More frequently, a chapter begins by calling attention to the gap in time that separates it from the preceding chapter: "un mes después de las escenas que acabamos de referir [. . .]." (335)

Once again, readers of *La voluntad* may recognize in this description an aspect of that novel's narrative structure, in which connecting time expressions are virtually omitted. Not one of the chapters of parts 1 or 2 begins with a time expression that could relate the chapter to the previous one. The most common temporal opening is *esta tarde*, although *hoy* is also used several times and *ayer* occasionally, without significant narrative linking to a "today." In part 3, only the opening of chapter 3—"Hace dos días que estoy en este convento" (264)—points to an extension of time beyond the chapter. In general, I would suggest that Martínez Ruiz's novelistic structure might be described as a radicalization of temporal aspects of *La Gaviota.*

The similarities between *La Gaviota* and *La voluntad* are not only formal. Thematically, the two novels share a number of common elements: the focus on provincial life, an emphasis on landscape, an ambitious artist protagonist (like the author) who finds this environment restricting and even stifling, a trip to the decadent capital by the protagonist which is ultimately disappointing, and a final return to provincial life to live in a marriage of oppressive mediocrity. And finally, each novel includes a self-conscious manifesto of its aesthetic premises. In *La Gaviota*, "se muestra a un grupo de personajes que en una tertulia aristocrática proyecta la elaboración de una novela de costumbres, «la novela por excelencia..., útil y agradable», obediente a los mismos principios determinantes de la que el lector está leyendo [. . .]" (Risco 74). In *La voluntad*, Azorín and Yuste also discuss their ideas about the novel. Well known is Yuste's dictum that "Lo que da la medida de un artista es su sentimiento de la naturaleza, del paisaje [. . .]" (130). Yuste also fulminates against descriptive practices that detract from verisimilitude, such as the use of comparisons—"Comparar es evadir la dificultad [. . .] una superchería que no debe emplear ningún artista" (130)—as well as excessively "literary" dialogue, and even the very presence of a plot: "Ante todo, no debe haber fábula... la vida no tiene fábula: es diversa, multiforme, ondulante, contradictoria [. . .]" (133). As in the case of *La Gaviota*, the novel in which these reflections take place in general conforms to the aesthetic criteria it promulgates.

With respect to Pereda's novel, I wish to focus on a number of elements that offer suggestive points of comparison with both *Paz en la guerra* and *Antonio Azorín*: the representation of the relationship between city and country, the narrative use of the journey, the novelistic structure and descriptive technique.

González Herrán, in his study of the theme of the city and the country in *Peñas arriba*, provides summaries of several literary models helpful for the study of the novel, which can also be useful in analyzing *Paz en la guerra* and the *Antonio Azorín* saga. The first is a type of nineteenth-century novel protagonized by what Lionell Trilling describes as the Young Man from the Provinces who goes to the capital. In this plot, a somewhat innocent although well read young man goes to the capital to seek his place in life (González 63). The second is a model proposed by Rodolfo Cardona as a complement to Trilling's: "Un Joven de la Capital [que] visita un lugar de provincia" (González 63). There, with his scientific education and modern values, he clashes, sometimes violently, with the local society. Often he becomes involved with the daughter of a prominent local family, "un hecho que les complica su vida psicológicamente, además de dificultar su acción. El Joven de la Capital desea efectuar un cambio en este ambiente provinciano, pero ya sea por falta de habilidad o por impotencia, sus planes no sólo le fallan, sino que termina siendo dominado por las fuerzas reaccionarias y perdiendo su propia vida" (González 64). Cardona sees the model described by Trilling as expressive of a conservative vision of society; the latter is more radical, as it "dramatiza la confrontación entre el progreso y la reacción" (González 64).

With respect to *Peñas arriba*, González Herrán observes that it presents the reader with "una variante del *pattern* que Car Dona diseña como modelo común de *Doña Perfecta*, *Padres e hijos* y *Tierras vírgenes*" (65) because here a young man from the city goes to the provinces, but instead of being aflame with a mission of bringing modernity to a backward society, and meeting a tragic end, he finds redemption, regeneration, and fulfillment (65). González Herrán sees in Pereda's attitudes toward city and country the fundamental paradigm of "Menosprecio de Corte y Alabanza de Aldea": "Pereda cree que es la vida cortesana, muelle, falsa y corrompida por el liberalismo, la que precisa regenerarse con la salva redentora de los pueblos como Tablanca" (65).

Within the narrative of the Young Man from the Capital who goes to the provinces, and its thematics of the city versus the country, González Herrán identifies the archetypal narrative of the hero's journey described by Joseph Campbell and modified by Juan Villegas in his study *La estructura mítica del héroe en la novela del siglo XX*:

> Sorprende advertir—escribe—que en numerosas obras literarias suele darse una situación básica similar: el protagonista descubre o hace evidente que el significado de su existencia no se satisface en su lugar de origen y que debe abandonarlo—generalmente por medio de un viaje, real o simbólico—y que luego de una sucesión de experiencias variadas llega a aceptar una forma de vida diferente o vuelve a su lugar inicial con una sabiduría que a veces pone al servicio de sus semejantes. (González 66-67)

González Herrán uses Campbell's narrative paradigm, and Villegas's amendments to accommodate it to the contemporary hero, here Marcelo, whose journey begins when he is summoned by his uncle's letters and during which he receives aid from various "helpers," ending with his integration into the rural society of Tablanca as its new patriarch.

The motivation for the protagonist's journey in *Antonio Azorín* is similar to that of Marcelo in *Peñas arriba*, as I will discuss further in the part of this chapter dedicated to Martínez Ruiz's second novel. In fact, it is the bidding of an uncle as well that motivates Ignacio's journey to his father's village in *Paz en la guerra.*[4] However, what I wish to point out here is that while the city-country conflict is central to both novels, both authors seem to invoke the paradigm of the journey only to subvert its linearity. The journeys in both novels are a constant *vaivén* with no place representing fulfillment or narrative closure. Ignacio moves from city street to mountain to village to battlefield, until he perishes in the last. His parents move back and forth from Villa to village without being able to find a resting place. Pachico goes to Madrid and back, and later to a small coastal town on the Cantabrian Ocean during the siege of Bilbao, without giving any sign of an inclination to settle. His life, presumably, will be a constant alternation between the heights and the urban lowlands.

Michael Ugarte has studied the constant traveling back and forth through "that expansive yet liminal space between the country town of Monóvar and Madrid" (158) which is a constant in Azorín's writing. For Ugarte these "frequent moves from the provinces to Madrid and vice versa are central to the process through which José Martínez Ruiz becomes Azorín" (159). Azorín's constant peregrinations are all "in search of something he simply will not find" (177).

García Castañeda has analyzed Marcelo's journey to Tablanca from another perspective: he observes parallels between Marcelo's first-hand account of his trip and the travel literature produced by European travelers to far-off lands. The principal similarity is that between the rhetorical strategies employed by nineteenth-century Spanish *costumbristas* and that

---

[4] The prevalence of uncle- and aunt-nephew relationships in turn-of-the-century narrative, especially in Unamuno but also in Baroja and Azorín, contrasted with the relative scarcity of parent-child relationships, is rather striking. It is possible that this configuration allows for a more flexible model of intergenerational relationships than that of parent- and especially father-child.

of contemporary travel writers to exotic, and especially colonial or post-colonial, countries:

> Si comparamos la actitud de muchos de estos viajeros con la de buena parte de nuestros escritores de costumbres pienso que algunos aspectos de las teorías críticas que hoy se aplican a la literatura de viajes pueden aplicarse también, hechas las salvedades pertinentes, a la de costumbres. Nuestros costumbristas fueron, en su mayoría, gente de la ciudad, educada y perteneciente a la burguesía que en su relación con los aldeanos y con las clases populares, objeto de su interés, adoptaron una actitud, semejante en más de un sentido, a la de aquellos viajeros. (141)

Pereda, a *costumbrista* before he was a novelist, makes use of this exoticizing optic to create a narrative strategy. The reader is invited to experience the rural society of inland Cantabria as the exotic place the city-dweller Marcelo finds it to be, at least initially. García Castañeda observes how Marcelo narrates his first contact with the village of Tablanca as "hechos acaecidos en un ambiente tan fascinante como desconocido" (142). In this way, García Castañeda points out, Marcelo, as traveler:

> está en una situación tópica del costumbrismo, la del ingenuo a quien sorprenden desconocidas costumbres. Desde tal perspectiva, como escribía Baquero Goyanes, el costumbrista ha de jugar a fingirse sorprendido por todo, y el efecto del pasmo podría resultar de una inadecuación o de un choque de perspectivas. (146)

This descriptive technique is also used by Unamuno in *Paz en la guerra* and, though somewhat less obviously, by Martínez Ruiz beginning with *La voluntad*. In *Paz en la guerra*, the most obvious example is that of Ignacio's initiation into rural life, and the strong impressions he receives. The characteristics of rural life are rendered here with a descriptive, almost lyrical intensity that is associated with the outsider's perspective on rural life.

Laín Entralgo called the writers and artists 1898 discoverers of Castile, noting that all of them brought the perspective of the "outsider" to their descriptions. It would seem that they also used their outsider's perspective to write about their native spaces.

Fernán Caballero and Pereda, like Azorín later, saw themselves as verbal artists. Fernán Caballero saw herself as a copyist of reality. Aguinaga Alfonso has noted Pereda's self-definition as painter:

> El escritor se llama a sí mismo *pintor.* En este sentido Pereda no hace más que continuar el tópico habitual de todos los escritores costumbristas desde Mesonero Romanos de quien Pereda se siente discípulo. El escritor montañés es continuador de sus maestros en el género y también hereda sus confusiones entre pintar y retratar. (30)

On the other hand, Montesinos has noted that Pereda's descriptions are sometimes weakened by the fact that he does not always describe from direct observation:

> Así, muchas de las descripciones de Pereda pueden ser excelentes páginas de prosa, pero no es imposible que nos defrauden por echar de menos en ellas lo que «pinta», justamente [. . .]. [E]l guía que nos lleva por la Montaña la conoce al dedillo y la siente hondamente, pero no siempre la ve porque *se la sabe.* El gran descriptor que pudo ser Pereda debería haber olvidado lo que había de encontrar ante sí cada día al abrir los postigos de su solana [. . .]. (264)

Montesinos also cites Pereda's poor grasp of color:

> Ese nimio detallismo es muy de la pintura española del tiempo; pero ocurre, como con esa misma pintura, que no es por lo brillante y original del color por lo que tal vez pueda interesarnos—y de

> hecho nos interesa poquísimo. Las manchas de color son raras en Pereda [. . .]. [N]o siente bien el color. (268-269)

It is where Pereda is deficient that Azorín will excel, cultivating a process of painstaking "annotation" from nature and developing an exceptional color vocabulary.

In summary, what I have tried to suggest here is that for the study of *Paz en la guerra*, *La voluntad* and *Antonio Azorín*, the regional novel and the *novela de costumbres* may provide models helpful for elucidating certain structural characteristics and descriptive techniques. With respect to the thematic and ideological content of the *novela de costumbres* and the regional novel, the differences that are observable between these and Azorín and Unamuno's early novels are as revealing as their similarities, as I shall discuss in the next section.

The intellectual and society in *Paz en la guerra* and *La voluntad*

Unamuno's intrahistoric landscape

It is virtually impossible to think of the rural subject in Unamuno's writings apart from his theory of *intrahistoria*, formulated in *En torno al casticismo* (1895). *Intrahistoria* is an eternal, unchanging space "underneath" the upheavals of history. Unamuno often uses the metaphor of water to describe the relationship between the two: "Una ola no es otra agua que otra, es la misma ondulación que corre por el mismo mar" (34). It is the anonymous, ordinary people, living out their lives beneath the drama of history, who embody the eternal continuity of this space: "En este mundo de los silenciosos, en este fondo del mar, debajo de la Historia, es donde vive la verdadera tradición, la eterna, en el presente, no en el pasado muerto para siempre y enterrado en cosas muertas" (34). The idea of intrahistoria, which Unamuno almost always expresses through natural metaphors and which is conceptualized largely in relation to the Castilian landscape, can be seen as a theory of landscape, as well as a metaphysical concept. A reading of Unamuno's presentation of nature and rural society in *Paz en la guerra* may help shed some light on the evolution of intrahistoria as a vision of landscape. In this novel, the intrahistoric vision is presented as the last in a series of other modes of envisioning nature, particularly the late Romantic and the nineteenth-century pastoral.

In *Paz en la guerra*, Unamuno describes the landscape around his native Bilbao from the point of view of Ignacio, the city-born son of an immigrant from the countryside. Ignacio begins his discovery of nature during his early adolescence, on weekend mountain escapes from his confining office apprenticeship and the disturbances of his newly awakened sexuality. In his descriptions of these excursions, Unamuno emphasizes Ignacio and his friends' experience of freedom in the mountains, which is contrasted to their life in the city:

> Entercábanse a trepar, sin apenas tomar aliento; llegaban a la cima, pesarosos de que no hubiese otra más alta allí cerca [. . .] [s]entían el placer de sudar, y como si con ello se les fueran los malos humores de la calle, y se renovaron por dentro. (166)

During Ignacio's first explorations of nature, rural society remains basically on the periphery of his consciousness. He and his friends' sense of difference as city boys is suggested by the way Juan José asks one owner of a *casería* where they have stopped on their way down from the mountain "un sinfin de preguntas, empeñado en demostrarle interés" (166). Descending home from these excursions at dusk, "a la hora de la oración, en que descansa la vista en dulce derretimiento de los colores" (174), among the impressions that emerge from the landscape are "un aldeano que apoyado en su laya les miraba desde la orilla del camino, ya otro que al cruzar les saludaba lentamente" (174). A slight sense of shyness, or aloofness, on the part of these villagers suggests that the estrangement between country- and city-dwellers is mutual.

However, these solitary rural figures blend with the peacefulness of the fading afternoon light to form a backdrop of late or post-Romantic tone that like that of some paintings by Joaquim Vayreda (1843-1894). The Romantic character of the scene is festively echoed when Rafael breaks into some verses of Zorrilla. This scene is the complement of mountain-top panoramas in a vision of nature which is predominantly Romantic, though unencumbered by serious reflection and updated with a certain appreciation for the hygienic, as well as spiritual, benefits of outdoor exercise, in line with the attitudes of the "Institutionists." Late or post-Romanticism, in literature and landscape, is the sign of Ignacio's early adolescence.

The second phase of Ignacio's initiation occurs when he travels to his father's village to attend a wedding. Ignacio is made conscious of his difference by his relatives, who receive him, though affectionately, as an outsider. Furthermore, his very limited command of the Basque language and many villagers' equally limited knowledge of Castilian impede communication. However, two important encounters during this visit enable Ignacio to feel more a part of this world. The first is his attraction to a village girl who sits across from him at the wedding banquet. The naturalness of the girl excites him, and his excitement becomes mixed with the sensuousness of the environment: "El vaho del campo le excitaba. Empezado el baile, bailó con frenesí, para sudar el deseo, con la aldeana de frente serena y los bovinos ojos, viéndola saltar ante él, sobre el fondo verde del campo" (218). As in the scene of his return from the mountains at dusk, the image of a villager blends with the natural environment, emphasizing a close link to nature, which is reinforced here by the animal imagery. However, unlike

Ignacio's mountain excursions, where his sweat is linked to escape from society, this phase of his initiation into rural life occurs under a social sign: family, the wedding, and the social rite of dance. The other "helper" Ignacio encounters during his stay in his father's village is Domingo, a laborer who will introduce him to the world of rural work. Through his affection for Domingo, and by participating in his labors, Ignacio's love of nature, awakened by his excursions into the mountains, becomes united to an appreciation for rural life.

Up to this point, Unamuno has invoked, in miniature, elements basic to nineteenth-century Spanish regional novels such *Pepita Jiménez* (1874) and *Peñas arriba* (1895). In these novels, an urban protagonist is able to integrate into rural life through a combination of relationship to a village patriarch, participation in village labor and/or sport, and marriage to a local woman. Unamuno includes these elements—a local masculine "helper," a potential bride, and family ties—but its conclusion, permanent integration, is rejected, and Ignacio returns to the city to participate in the imminent war.

It is also in this part of the novel where the narrator, going beyond Ignacio's point of view, begins to describe the village in terms of the intrahistoric. In this village, where industrialization has not yet intruded, and "[t]ampoco se había roto para ellos el primitivo nexo entre la producción y el consumo" (220), the villagers live face to face with life, "tomándola en serio y con sencillez, sin intención segunda ni reflexión alguna, espontáneamente, esperando, sin pensar apenas en tal esperanza, otra, arrullados por el campo en un canto silencioso, como canto de cuna para la muerte" (221). It is in this world that Ignacio's parents will take refuge after their son's death in the war, but the real heir to this intrahistoric vision will be Pachico, Unamuno's alter ego, the final protagonist of the book.

Pachico, up until now, has been a marginal presence in the novel. An intellectual who has studied in Madrid, and who has lost the religious faith of his childhood, Pachico is a skeptical, distanced observer of the events that unfold around him. A passing friend of Ignacio, Pachico took pleasure in unnerving the naively impassioned young Carlist. Yet, during the war, Pachico's intellectual battles begin to yield to an awareness of life around him. He frequents cafés where "[c]ada uno de los concurrentes a aquel cafetín tenía carácter propio, insustituible, como cada hijo de vecino" (443). He is also drawn to the countryside with new interest. He still has his intellectual obsessions, but "por debajo de aquellas refriegas mentales palpitábale inmenso y oscuro el mundo de las pacíficas impresiones, de las humildes imágenes de las cosas cotidianas, continuo sustento de su mente" (445-46). Pachico's awakening to the reality of intrahistoria, of life "below," will be intensified by Ignacio's death, which he privately and sincerely grieves. Pachico reflects on the meaning of Ignacio's lost life and questions whether it is completely lost after all, since "[t]ales vidas son la atmósfera espiritual de un pueblo, la que respiramos todos y a todos nos sustenta y espiritualiza" (447). The intellectual Pachico and the intrahistoric subject, Ignacio, coexist in invisible interdependence.

Having finally completed his own initiation into nature with a mountaintop experience of harmony and freedom, Pachico rejects a life of contemplative retirement and returns to the city:

> Allí arriba la contemplación serena le da resignación trascendente y eterna, madre de la irresignación temporal, del no contentarse jamás aquí abajo, del pedir siempre mayor salario; y baja decidido a provocar en los demás el descontento, primer motor de todo progreso y de todo bien. (510)

Pachico has finally found an altruistic purpose for his ability to disquiet others. Lily Litvak, in a study of the influence of

Ruskin's ethics and aesthetics in Unamuno's early work, sees in this ending confirmation that Unamuno, like Ruskin, saw beauty as having a moral dimension. Pachico's experience of natural beauty is not an end in itself, but an inspiration to work for the improvement of life for all people (*Ruskin* 219-20).

During his descent to the city, Pachico, pausing "a saludar a algún labriego que brega con la tierra esquiva, piensa en cuán gran parte es esta obra del hombre, que, humanizando a la naturaleza, la sobrenaturaliza poco a poco" (510). The worker's labor parallels the future that Pachico has proposed for himself: to struggle without ceasing to make human society a little divine. The idea that the intellectual's existence parallels that of the intrahistoric subject is also suggested by the juxtaposition of Pedro Antonio's submersion in the intrahistoric world, in which he finally finds peace, with Pachico's simultaneous growing awareness of this world. The difference is that Pedro Antonio's experience is mostly affective, while Pachico's has a rational, even metaphysical component. Pedro Antonio's contact with intrahistoric reality is a yielding to sleep and dream; Pachico's is an awakening.

The notion of a parallel, though hierarchical relationship between the intellectual and the intrahistoric subject is even more apparent in Unamuno's essay "Brianzuelo de la Sierra" in *Paisajes*. In this essay, Unamuno recounts a trip in which he disconcerts his traveling companion by stating that he would prefer to stay in his room at the inn and *soñar* (41) the town that he has not yet seen. Later, Unamuno and his friend meet an old village woman who seems to be staring out over the valley from her doorway. Although she gives the strangers accurate information about a town in the distance, she is, in fact, blind. As Unamuno has predicted, she knows the landscape by heart. She remembers it "como si lo viera" (43). Here, Unamuno's preference for imaginative vision, expressed that morning, connects him to the intrahistoric villager. However, the fact that

Unamuno's preference to imagine the landscape is willed while the woman's need to imagine is imposed by her blindness, together with his rather condescending theorizing about the townspeople to his friend and the woman's respectful attitude toward the gentlemen from the city (70), indicates that the analogy is hierarchical.

Unamuno's final privileging, in *Paz en la guerra*, of this ethical vision of nature, which is linked to his concept of the intrahistoric world, implies a partial rejection of the two artistic visions of nature he has invoked earlier in the novel, the Romantic and the rural-pastoral, although elements of each are assimilated into the intrahistoric landscape. Though it may seem somewhat paradoxical—given that one of the defining characteristics of the intrahistoric world is its unchanging, eternal character—by presenting this vision within the novel as the last in a succession of earlier landscape aesthetics, Unamuno gives the intrahistoric landscape a history.

Pachico's final mountaintop vision is only apparently one of a landscape without figures because collective, intrahistoric life, symbolized by Ignacio's "transformation," has been metaphorically incorporated into its very atmosphere. Blanco Aguinaga writes that one of the important influences on Unamuno's early social thought was Spencer, "whose idea of progress is inseparable from 'organic' evolution," one consequence of which is that "death is denied importance, being nothing but a transformation of matter from which new forms will issue" (48). Through the linking of death, birth, nature, intrahistoria, and atmosphere in *Paz en la guerra*, Unamuno's landscape becomes a cosmic space in which all life, past and present, endures in a form of vital energy. Still, this vision of nature, with all its ideological implications—seen from "above" as opposed to experienced from "below"—is the privilege of Pachico/Unamuno, the intellectual, and therefore, while Unamuno's vision of nature is linked to progressive ideals, it also reinforces the hierarchical division between the observing subject and the "other" in the landscape.

Martínez Ruiz and the elusive "other"

La voluntad, like *Paz en la guerra*, can be read as an intellectual *bildungsroman*, or perhaps more accurately, as an *anti-bildungsroman*, since the protagonist's experiences fail to result in the formation of a solid identity. Antonio Azorín is a young writer and intellectual, discontent with society and struggling to form an independent ideological and aesthetic identity. Like Pachico prior to his determination to take up the struggle for progress and social reform, Azorín, though of anarchist leanings, suffers from a lack of positive ideals. The various ideological options that he encounters through books, friends, and mentors fail to ignite more than a passing enthusiasm, and the result is a painful state of inertia. Perhaps even more than in Pachico's case in *Paz en la guerra*, a major dimension of Azorín's conflict is his isolation from the society in which he lives, the vast majority of which is socially and ideologically "other" to the young, middle-class intellectual. This theme is a constant in the novel, although often subtly presented.

At the beginning of the novel, Azorín appears to exist in almost complete isolation from the society of the small, provincial city where he lives, in a largely agricultural region of Levantine Spain. Conspicuously absent or suppressed is any mention of family, and Azorín thus appears to lack even this most basic link to society. Immersed in his books, Azorín's only regular companion is his friend and mentor, Yuste. Yuste and Azorín are misfits in the town, two "espíritus avanzados, progresivos, radicales," whose "secreta reacción contra la idea fija" (95) disquiets the people around them. Unable to grasp these subtle personalities, the good citizens of Yecla react with "la irritación que es la del niño que no entiende el mecanismo de un juguete y lo rompe" (95), and the "buenas devotas" (95) sigh and shake their heads. This incomprehension seems to bother Azorín little, and is even a source of pride: "Azorín no hace gran caso de estos suspiros piadosos y continúa hablando con el maestro y leyendo sus libros grandes y pequeños" (95).

Azorín's isolation is reinforced through the novel's relative suppression of the fictional world. Unlike the minutely detailed worlds of nineteenth-century realist novels, the broader fictional world of *La voluntad* appears only sporadically, in fragments that are often too selective to allow the reader to effectively reconstruct a "world." This relative thinness of the fictional world is a consequence of the prevalence of discursive over descriptive language, which is a feature of what Roberta Johnson calls the early twentieth-century Spanish philosophical novel. The writers of these novels, which include Baroja, Martínez Ruiz, and Unamuno, "invented a novelistic mode that is more self-conscious about its philosophical purpose than are most novels. In their version of the philosophical novel, ideas are evident to the reader in an immediate rather than latent way. [. . .] [They] think and talk about life in the abstract as much as or more than they live it" (5-6). One result of the prevalence of discursive language in these novels is the proportionate reduction of their narrative dimension: "Often these novels contain just as much story potential as other works on the same theme, but the more philosophically transparent novel refuses to flesh out its story" (6). Another consequence is a relative thinness of the fictional world, because, in Martínez-Bonati's terms, discursive language is relatively weak in illocutionary force (Johnson 79). In the case of *La voluntad*, the scarcity of the fictional world also functions to underscore the protagonist's isolation from the society in which he lives, which remains at the margins, evoked but only partially revealed. *La voluntad*'s resistance to "fleshing out" its fictional world is evident from an examination of its prologue and opening scenes.

The prologue recounts the vicissitudes of the construction of Yecla's new church through historical documentation of the project. This technique of drawing from primary historical documents and statistics to evoke a past reality that Azorín used in *Los hidalgos* (1900) and *El alma castellana* (1900) to write about seventeenth- and eighteenth-century Spain, is used here to evoke a more recent event, the rather anachronistic construction of a grandly scaled church initiated by a "pueblo fervoroso" (57) in the nineteenth century. Andrés Amorós has observed that this prologue, which is like a "pórtico" to the novel, delays the reader's full immersion into the novel's fictional world (343), which, as we have said, even within the body of the novel never attains the fullness of the world of a nineteenth-century realist novel.

It is in the prologue that a member of Yecla's laboring class first appears. He is *el Mudico*, the last and lowest paid of the list of boys contracted for general labor during the phase of construction that resumes, after a gap, in 1847. *El Mudico* disappears from the roster after scarcely a week of work, prompting the narrator to reflect upon his fate: "Y yo pienso en este pobre niño despreciado, que durante una semana trae humildamente la ofrenda de sus fuerzas á la gran obra, y luego desaparece, acaso muere" (57). The understated pathos of this passage is important. In *La voluntad*, Martínez Ruiz abstains from overt sentimentalization of the lower classes found in rural novels such as Valera's *Doña Luz*, Fernán Caballero's *Clemencia*, Pereda's *Peñas arriba*, or even Blasco Ibáñez's *La barraca*.

In the opening descriptions of Yecla, various members of the town's laboring class are described. Following the initial panoramic vision of the city and the surrounding countryside at dawn, the impersonal narrator turns his attention to the waking city, although in this scene the human dimension is largely suppressed in favor of architecture. Nevertheless, some images of ordinary Yeclans do filter through. These descriptions, while minimal, accentuate their subjects' inwardness and opacity with relation to the observer: "En las aceras, un viejo teje pleita ensimismado; una mujer inclinada sobre aceitosa cabellera va repasándola hebra por hebra" (63). In the new part of the city, "grupos de devotas [. . .] cuchichean en una esquina" (64) and "labriegos enfundados en amarillentas cabazas largas" pass by in silence. In the beginning of chapter IV, where the collective life of the city is again the subject, "tras las vidrieras diminutas, manchas rosadas, pálidas, cárdenas de caras femeninas, miran con ojos ávidos o se inclinan sobre su trabajo" (75). Each of these figures, either by virtue of their physical position, their apparel, or their low voices, is partially invisible or inaudible to the observer. Each individual or group seems to be a small, private world, turning on its own axis. On the one hand, the isolation in which these Yeclans are presented symbolizes the state of generalized social isolation in Yecla. In the epilogue, Martínez Ruiz ruefully remarks that "aquí, en un pueblo, cada uno se encierra en su casa, liado en su capa, junto a la lumbre, y deja morirse de inanición al vecino" (299). But with respect to Azorín, "un raro" in the town, isolated in his books, communicating only with Yuste, these muted images have a special resonance: the ordinary people of Yecla are as opaque to Azorín as he is to them.

To understand Martínez Ruiz's presentation of the laboring class in *La voluntad*, a passage from *Diario de un enfermo* (1901) is suggestive. E. Inman Fox describes *Diario de un enfermo* as a pre-text, and perhaps even an early attempt to write *La voluntad*.

> En esta pre-novela, pues, encontramos la historia íntima, en forma de diario, de un hombre que medita angustiosamente sobre la

> inanidad de la lucha vital y de un escritor que no puede reconciliar la contemplación de la vida y la participación activa en ella: la antinomia entre vida e inteligencia que vemos luego en el protagonista Antonio Azorín. (25)

In *Diario de un enfermo*, the working class of Madrid is identified with the "life" that eludes the narrator. One day, the lonely writer hears music coming from a carpentry shop across the street where a dance is taking place (172). He pauses for a moment in the doorway, watching the dancers:

> [P]asaban y repasaban las parejas, juntos, apretados, el bailador y la bailadora, el brazo de *él* ceñido al talle de *ella*, la cabeza de *ella* yacente en el hombro de *él*; jadeantes ambos, los ojos resplandecientes, los cuerpos lacios [...]. Y yo aquí leyendo filosofías... ¿Dónde está la vida: en los libros o en la calle? (173)

Here, Azorín's bourgeois envy of the "vitality" of working-class society is manifested as eroticism.

In *La voluntad*, the life force Azorín longs for is projected onto a woman—"lo eterno femenino" —who, like him, is a member of the landowning class, and thus a socially appropriate object of desire. Iluminada is described as "una fuerza libre de la Naturaleza, como el agua que salta y susurra, como la luz, como el aire" (184). But Azorín's eventual marriage to her is a disaster precisely because it locks him into a class structure that he finds abhorrent and suffocating. The transgressive longing suggested by the scene of the dance in *Diario del enfermo* is apparently absent in *La voluntad*, but the novel's unhappy ending suggests that the conflict between "vida e inteligencia" has at least something to do with the oppressiveness of class. The absence of identification between the working classes and "real life" in *La voluntad* is only apparent.

The Spanish laboring class is often the subject, implicit or explicit, of many of the discursive passages in the novel, mediated principally by Yuste and Azorín. The use of situated speech, Johnson observes, "offered early twentieth-century Spanish writers an opportunity to explore a variety of ideas without making the kind of commitment to one philosophical position required by journalistic or philosophical prose" (7). Therefore, no single ideology is unconditionally endorsed, nor can any be interpreted as an unequivocal expression of the author's views, even when these ideas are known to have been shared by the author. In addition to the noncommittal distance afforded by situated speech, the writer sometimes ironizes his character's speech further with additional information that undermines or contradicts what a character says. This is especially true in the case of Yuste.

Yuste's speech dominates the first part of the novel to such an extent that Fox has claimed that "[e]n realidad, Antonio Azorín no existe en la primera parte de la novela" (33). For example, in chapter 5, Yuste advances ideas that "siguen al pie de la letra la ideología anárquico-comunista de Pedro Kropotkin y Sebastian Faure" (Fox 84). "La propiedad es el mal," announces Yuste, and therefore "nada más natural, nada más justo, nada más humano que destruir la propiedad" (80). However, the violence of Yuste's words are contrasted by the narrator's description of "la placidez de este anochecer de Agosto" (80) as the two friends set out on their daily walk through Yecla's surrounding countryside. The irony of the juxtaposition of Yuste's rhetoric with the calm, motionless landscape is reinforced at the end of the chapter when: "el maestro, calmado con la apacibilidad de la noche, sonrió, satisfecho de su pintoresca asociación de ideas" (84).

The meaning of the ironic contrast between Yuste's social discourse and his tranquil surroundings becomes clear in chapter 8, when the narrator declares: "Este buen maestro—¡habrá que confesarlo!—es, en el fondo, un burgués redomado" (98). Following this comment by the narrator, Azorín and Yuste set out on another walk: "Así, esta tarde, que hace hermoso sol y los árboles ya verdean con los retoños primaverales, hubiera sido una crueldad privarle al maestro de su paseo" (98). The landscape is one more aspect of his middle-class identity, a cherished habit like his ubiquitous snuff, and a temptation to complacency and inaction.

The sincerity of Yuste's progressive ideas is also put into question by references to his egotism. Small slights or flattering attentions affect his social convictions in the moment. Yuste's particularly vehement speech in chapter 5 is partly brought on by the omission of his name in an article in which all of his old friends appear (82). And in chapter 10, Yuste is unable to empathize with Azorín's fury over Puche's destructive intervention in his relationship with Justina, because "una carta de uno de los más brillantes escritores de la gente nueva, que principia así: 'Maestro'" (115) has left him in a splendid mood. When Azorín goes to Yuste's study "para significarle su incondicional adhesión" (115), Yuste surprises him by instead advising patience. Citing a newspaper article by Tolstoy on a recent peasant uprising in Seville, in which he expresses disagreement with this course of action—"No es el camino de la violencia el que nos conducirá a la paz deseada; es la misma paz, o mejor, la rebeldía pasiva" (177) —Yuste concurs: "Estas son las palabras de un hombre sabio y de un hombre bueno... Así, con dulzura, con la resignación, con la pasividad es cómo ha de venir a la tierra el reinado de la justicia" (118).

Yuste's isolation from the real men and women for whom he alternately exhorts violence or passivity is clear in chapter 24, which recounts Yuste and Azorín's last afternoon together in the Yeclan countryside. At Iluminada's family's house in El Pulpillo, Yuste and Azorín sit down beside *el abuelo*, the father of the current tenant. No longer able to work in the fields, el abuelo spends his time by the fire, engaged in sedentary tasks and caring for his granddaughter. As if the old farmer were not even there, Yuste launches into speculations on "el porvenir de toda esta clase labradora, que es el sostén del Estado, y ha sido, en realidad, la base de la civilización occidental" (175), and whose current way of life will inevitably be destroyed by the approaching "gran transformación social" (176). During this speech, el abuelo remains silent: "[S]us manos se mueven incesantemente tejiendo el esparto. Sus ojuelos brilladores miran de cuando en cuando a Yuste, y una ligera sonrisa asoma a sus labios" (176). The irony of this situation is pointed. With the silent presence of the old laborer and his slyly mocking smile, Martínez Ruiz ironizes bourgeois intellectualizing, progressive or not, about a social class from which they are so fundamentally isolated.

The conclusion of Yuste's speech further reveals his ideas about class. Speaking of the transformation to come, Yuste recognizes that some of the things he most cherishes will also be destroyed in the process. Art for art's sake will cease to exist: "El arte debe *servir* para la obra humanitaria, debe ser *útil*... es decir, es un *medio*, y no un *fin*" (177). History, "el más aristocrático de los gustos" (177), may not even exist in the future. It makes Yuste sad to think that these things, "que son las más altas de la humanidad," will be "maltratadas en esta terrible palingenesia, que será muy fecunda en otras cosas, también muy altas, y muy humanas, y muy justas" (177). Yuste thus establishes an implicit parallel between the rural workers and himself, through the suffering that both will have to undergo for the sake of social transformation. Both will lose things that are dear to them (a way of life for the workers, a humanistic but class-based conception of art for Yuste's), for the sake of a future good. However, like the parallels that Unamuno establishes in *Paz en la guerra* between Pachico and the "intrahistoric" laborers, Yuste's implicit analogy between himself and the rural working class reproduces a hierarchical relationship.

Furthermore ironic is the fact that Azorín, who represents the younger generation, appears unable to break free from the prejudices and limitations that beset the previous one, represented by Yuste. Away from Yuste's shadow, Azorín's critical impulses seem to stir. Alone in his study, reading his beloved Montaigne, Azorín reflects on the sadness of Spanish small-town life: "El peligro de la vida de pueblo es que se siente uno vivir [. . .]" (96). However, these reflections are the product of solitary reading, not experience. Azorín does not make the leap from his meditations to observed life (as Martínez Ruiz will in *Los pueblos* [1904]). By the end of the chapter, the stimulation he has received from his reading of Montaigne becomes discomfort, and Azorín rushes back to Yuste for relief from his depressed mood, "que era como salir de un hoyo para caer en una fosa" (97).

It has already been mentioned how, in the beginning of chapter 11, Azorín's private emotions affect his public convictions, in this way mirroring Yuste. However, at the end of this chapter, Azorín confronts his mentor with unprecedented violence on the subject of resignation, provoked by Yuste's comments on Tolstoy's article: "¡No, no! ¡Eso es indigno, eso es inhumano, eso es bochornoso!" (118). Azorín considers passivity before violence to be the most immoral attitude one can have. Furthermore, he questions Tolstoy's apparent ingenuity in this article. "Tolstoi mismo, ¿puede asegurar que no ha armado con sus libros el brazo de un obrero en rebelión? El libro, la palabra, el discurso... ¡pero eso es ya acción!" (118). Here, Azorín directly pits himself against the previous generation, and furthermore, he implicitly equates his own activities as a young journalist with positive action and even with violent rebellion. However, the merit of this claim is implicitly questioned through its juxtaposition with the account of the failure of Quijano's dynamite-carrying explosive in chapter 13. As the journalists, the townspeople, and the inventor himself follow the successive tests, their initial excitement slowly deflates:

> Los espectadores se diseminan entre las viñas. Reina un momento de silencio. Y la negra tabla parte revolando como un murciélago. Luego se disparan nueve más . . . . Los periodistas se aburren; a lo lejos el profesor de Artes y Ciencias—un señor de traje negro y botas blancas—se da golpecitos en la pierna con un sarmiento. (127)

Azorín's ardent language in chapter 11 seems likewise to fizzle out without consequence, and in fact he is obliged to write the obituary for the experiment whose success he had passionately predicted in the local paper.

While this juxtaposition suggests that Azorín, for all his rebellious passion, is perhaps no more effective than Yuste, a closer reading of chapters 12 and 13 reveals that a shift has in fact taken place after their argument. This shift is reflected in the presentation of the landscape. Chapter 12 is virtually pure description, the second extensive landscape description after the opening panoramic vision of Yecla. The latter is characterized by rigorous, almost photographic objectivity. There is no clear mood, only a setting and a rhythm of life. In chapter 12, however, the landscape is alive, febrile, teeming: "En este rojo anochecer de agosto el cielo parece inflamarse con las pasiones de la ciudad enardecida" (122). For the first time in the novel, the landscape is employed to express the collective mood of its populace.

In chapter 13, the landscape is reduced again to a setting that appears in only a few images. Yet these images, cited earlier, are revealing. The crowd disperses "entre las viñas" (127). The bored professor "se da golpecitos en la pierna con un sarmiento" (127). The grape, evoked here twice, is a symbol of Yecla's decadence, as will become clear in part 3, chapter 4, when Azorín discusses the impact of the treaty with France of 1882 to 1892. What in the later chapter is the subject of discourse is here prefigured in an image, through which the failed experiment is subtly linked to Yecla's history and economy—its environment, in sum. If in chapter 12 we see the beginnings of a more anthropomorphized landscape, in chapter 13 we get the beginnings of a critical or ethical vision of landscape, as Elena Jongh-Rossel calls it (74).

From chapter 12 on, the landscape tends to reflect Azorín's emotional state, or his emerging critical vision. It is immediately following upon these two chapters that we find the famous passage in which Yuste declares that "[lo] que da la medida de un gran artista es su sentimiento de la naturaleza, del paisaje" (130). This passage alerts the reader that to appreciate the full significance of discourse in the novel, he must also attend to the description of the landscapes in which it is situated. In an 1904 article, "La filosofía de Pío Baroja," Azorín concludes that the search for a coherent philosophy in Baroja's novels is futile: "[E]l mismo valor tiene tal artículo que tal otro, o este o el otro teorema" (85). Rather, the "fuerza extraordinaria del novelista" lies in "la intensa emoción de estas visiones y paisajes, que sobre *tal fondo de filosofía* implacable, aparecen rápidas al pasar las páginas" (*Los pueblos. La Andalucía trágica y otros artículos [1904-1905]* 85, emphasis mine). The usual concept of landscape as background is explicitly inverted.

The landscape in *La voluntad* is not, however, uniform. At least five kinds of landscapes appear, although they overlap somewhat: 1) the hyper-objective, photographic landscape (ex. p.1, ch.1); 2) the landscape settings of Yuste's monologues, classical, humanist, throughout part I; 3) the critical, or ethical landscape (ex. p.1, ch.13 and p.3, ch.6); 4) the determinist landscape, which resembles the critical landscape, but whose language is more densely poetic (ex. p.1, ch.15 and p.2, ch.3-4); and 5) the expressionist landscape, which is the most abstract, subjective, and poetic, with an emphasis on a mood or state of mind (p. 1, ch.12 and especially ch. 29; beg. p.3, ch.6). This last type of landscape may be related to that which appears in the background of the photograph of Bécquer that Azorín contemplates at the National Library (253).

While Azorín's deepening interiority and his development of critical vision are implied in the novel, Azorín's narrative in *La voluntad* is still an *anti-bildungsroman*. Like Yuste, Azorín remains trapped in his excessive intellectualizing, although he struggles with it in part 3. And like Yuste, Azorín is completely isolated from the society around him, particularly from the lower classes. Although his experience in Madrid seems to free him up somewhat to observe the life around him—in the streets, in and from the train—there is still no contact, no direct communication. In Toledo, he overhears "un místico en la vida, no en los libros, un místico que es un pobre labrador castellano que habla con la sencillez y elegancia de un Fray Luis de León" (206), but no direct interaction with him is reported.

Azorín's marriage to Iluminada at the end of the novel results in even greater social isolation. In the last chapter of part 3, Azorín momentarily evokes the prospect of a happy ending in marriage. Sitting outside the chapel with Iluminada after mass, Azorín recounts that "nos ponemos a hablar un rato con los campesinos" (283). This comment is the first allusion to direct communication between Azorín and members of the laboring class in the novel. Father Ortuño teases Azorín, the villagers laugh, and the reticent young man admits that he laughs, too. We seem suddenly in the midst of a regional novel: the rural setting, the church, the apparent harmony between landowners and their subjects, an upcoming wedding, family. However, at the end of this scene Azorín disappears abruptly as a narrator. In the letters of "Martínez Ruiz" that form the epilogue, Azorín is presented as radically changed, miserable, virtually inert in an atmosphere of stifling provincialism. Rather than integrating him into an idyllic rural society, marriage makes him the enemy of the laborers, whom he is unable to help because his wife has sole control of their estate. The landscape disappears entirely.

Roberta Johnson reads this ending as a rebuke to Pío Baroja for failing "to find a non-bourgeois resolution to his protagonist's quandary" (85) in *Camino de perfección*. Perhaps Martínez Ruiz's ultimate criticism of Azorín's marriage is the change of style he employs for the epilogue. Martínez Ruiz's letters are written in the style of a realist novel, the very model from which he was trying to break in *La voluntad*. Viewed through this ideological lens, Azorín is as opaque, as nearly invisible, as the laboring classes that inhabit the margins of the novel.

In conclusion, *Paz en la guerra* and *La voluntad* are perhaps the first Spanish novels to thematize in a serious way the particular contradictions and obstacles confronting the "first, first-rate intellectuals of the bourgeois vanguard who tried to cross over to the enemy" (Blanco Aguinaga 38). In *Paz en la guerra*, Unamuno provides a "solution" to his protagonist's existential conflict through the introduction of a vision of socio-historic reality in which nature becomes a unifying space and a motivation to altruistic action, although a hierarchical division between the observing intellectual subject and the "other" in the landscape is preserved. Martínez Ruiz rejects, for the moment, any lasting solution to his protagonist's isolation, his fruitless intellectualizing and the limitations of his middle-class identity, while dramatizing the intensity of this struggle.

Narrative subversions in *Antonio Azorín*

The first problem for the reader of *Antonio Azorín* who has already read *La voluntad* is that of the continuity, or discontinuity, of the character Antonio Azorín between the two novels. Ugarte observes that:

> Like Antonio Azorín—the self-created facsimile of Martínez Ruiz—the new novel mentioned at the culmination of *La voluntad* ("la segunda vida de Antonio Azorín," [the second life of Antonio Azorín, 300]), is a direct reference to something real. It is the text of *Antonio Azorín*, the second volume in the series of novels dealing with the life of Martínez Ruiz's model of himself. Yet this is not necessarily the continuation of Antonio Azorín's life from the point at which the author left him at the end of *La voluntad*. The life of Antonio Azorín does not follow conventional chronological patterns, another indication that time is for Martínez Ruiz an abstraction, while place is the raw material of his writing. (174)

Fox points out that any attempt to see in the Antonio Azorín of the two novels a reflection of the author's linear development "desde una personalidad agresiva, periodista militante, a un sensitivo escéptico que da transcendencia al detalle" (Fox, *Introducción*15), is complicated by the fact that, despite its publication date, *Antonio Azorín* may have been at least partly written contemporaneously with the earlier *Diario de un enfermo*.[5]

Besides the problem of the continuity of character between the two novels, there is also one of form. Fox considers *Antonio Azorín* inferior to *La voluntad* as a novel:

> Empieza como una novela de interesantes posibilidades, pero se deshace hacia los últimos capítulos. En realidad Martínez Ruiz no la termina; [...] los últimos capítulos de la tercera parte son colaboraciones periodísticas escritas para otras ocasiones y simplemente agregadas al final del libro. (21)

He furthermore observes that the "yo" that emerges in these articles, and which substitutes the earlier third-person narrator,

[5] See Fox *Introducción*, esp. pp. 16-21.

is "el yo tan común en los artículos del periódico de Martínez Ruiz" (Fox 1992, 21-22). Sobejano has studied this phenomenon in *Las confesiones*, in which the pieces of the second part detach from the chronological structure of the first part.[6]

With regard to understanding the novel's structure, I would like to propose once again that a comparison to *Peñas arriba* may be helpful. In contrast to Marcelo's dramatic move from fashionable urban life to a rural, agricultural community, *Antonio Azorín* presents a meandering journey from the small town of Monóvar to the small city of Petrel, followed by excursions to other locations—Alicante, Villena, Orihuela—and finally to Madrid. However, *Antonio Azorín* presents some marked similarities to Pereda's novel. In both narratives, the protagonist is shown initially as somewhat idle and undirected. While Marcelo leads a life of urban distractions, Azorín is enrapt in the observation of the minutia of his natural and social environment. While these activities are not pernicious, they seem to lack focus, and the energy of these early scenes is somewhat languid. The journey to visit his uncle will be the first purposeful, energetic gesture that the protagonist shows. As in *Peñas arriba*, a journey is set in motion when an ailing uncle summons the protagonist with a letter urging him to visit. Marcelo is an orphan, while Azorín, as in *La voluntad*, in an apparent orphan by default, since parents are never mentioned. A description of the journey ensues, although not as minutely related as Marcelo's arduous trip to Tablanca in *Peñas arriba*. As in the latter, a description of the uncle's house serves as an architectural reflection of its owner's personality and values, synthesized in the opening words: "La casa de Verdú es ancha, clara, limpia" (123). While Pascual Verdú is far from the

---

[6] See Sobejano, Gonzalo. "Baudelaire entre José Martínez Ruiz y Azorín." *Homenaje a Elena Catena*. Madrid: Castalia, 2001.

patriarch of *Peñas arriba*, he nonetheless imprints some of the values he represents on his young nephew. In fact, Martínez Ruiz dedicates to him one of the most affectionate tributes in any of his books: "[E]s un bello ejemplar de esos hombres-fuerzas que cantan, ríen, se apasionan, luchan, caen en desesperaciones hondas, se exaltan en alegrías súbitas [. . .] que son buenos, son sencillos, que son grandes" (125).

Like Marcelo, Azorín has a helper, Sarrió, who facilitates his entry into the community. Furthermore, Azorín develops an attachment to a local girl, in this case Sarrió's daughter Pepita. Although he does not marry her, this sentimental interlude suggests the protagonist's desire, if ambivalent, for integration and belonging. It is precisely the subversion of the conventional generic conclusion—marriage and integration—that seems to induce an act of writing. In Azorín's letters to Pepita from Madrid, the protagonist's "yo" emerges for the first time in the novel. Furthermore, various elements of these letters, such as the author's self-representation in his surroundings and the careful description of these for an absent reader, are constant features of his travel writings.

The archetypal journey summarized by González Herrán is common to both Pereda's *Peñas arriba* and Martínez Ruiz's *La voluntad* and *Antonio Azorín*. However, while Pereda uses the narrative paradigm to bring steadily paced drama to his narrative, Martínez Ruiz uses the journey to excite certain expectations, some of which are fulfilled and some of which are frustrated, giving an element of narrative unpredictability to the author's writings, despite the scarcity of traditional plot. By exploiting expectations attached to these conventions, Azorín creates small dramatic pulses that partly compensate for the lack of an overarching plot.

With respect to the treatment of landscape, *Antonio Azorín* does depart, in part 3, from that of *La voluntad*. As Fox notes, the extensive opening landscape descriptions are strikingly similar to those of *La voluntad.* Similar, too, is the determinist and sociological perspective in the descriptions of the various places Azorín visits with Sarrió. As Lily Litvak has studied, these descriptions provide evidence that Azorín did not necessarily see the small town as his ideal environment, in opposition to the large city, but rather towns and medium-sized cities that "are prosperous and that show a strong vitality, developing organically and integrating harmoniously the modern with the old" (Litvak, *Azorín's anti-Urban Philosophy* 294).

It is really in part 3 that a new vision of landscape emerges, and most of all in Antonio Azorín's letters to Pepita. Azorín's letters from Madrid to Pepita are among the first examples of Azorín's urbane, poetic vision applied to a mixture of urban and provincial content. The mixture emerges as Azorín evokes Petrel, naturally connected to Pepita, from his urban setting: "Tu recuerdo es para mí algo muy grato en medio de esta aridez de Madrid. [. . .] Escríbeme: dime si paseáis por la plaza al anochecer, mientras suena la fuente y el cielo se va poniendo fosco; dime si salís a las huertas y os sentáis bajo esa nogueras anchas, espesas, redondas" (172). The pieces are characterized by an intimate tone and clear affection for his reader. Like the anonymous reader in Alicante, Pepita is a consumer of Azorín's literature who is outside the realm of intellectuals and artists, yet it is to her that Azorín seems comfortable revealing his private self.

In these letters we begin to see Azorín's sense of sympathy with his environment. The bells of the neighboring church are his friends in the city. "Las cosas son como los hombres" he tells his friend (174), and "Es la voz de esta iglesia, que suplica a los hombres un poco de piedad" (175). Unlike the extensive descriptions of place that begin both *La voluntad* and *Antonio Azorín*, these descriptions are written for a clear reader, one who is both sympathetic and an object of affection. It seems to be the invoked presence of Pepita that facilitates the development of a more intimate tone. Description becomes an expression of connection between reader and writer. While there is no explicit reader in *Las confesiones*, *Los pueblos*, or *La ruta de Don Quijote*, there is often an intimate tone similar to that in the letters to Pepita. I would suggest that this intimate tone, which is the mark of some of Azorín's best-known pages on landscape, rests in a changed vision of the relationship between reader and writer. Azorín now hopes not only to express ideas and vision, but also to establish a relationship of cordial sympathy with his unknown readers.

Chapter Two

First contact: landscape as formative influence

After writing their early novels, both Unamuno and Azorín turned to the memoir form. *Recuerdos de niñez y de mocedad* (1908) and *Las confesiones de un pequeño filósofo* (1904) are part of their projects of self-creation and self-definition as intellectuals and writers. The memoirs are like short prequels of sorts to the novelistic selves of *Paz en la guerra* (and to an extent *Nuevo mundo*), and *La voluntad* and *Antonio Azorín.* In this chapter I will concentrate on the sections of these memoirs that relate to the authors' early experiences of landscape.

The childhood experiences of nature that Unamuno recalls in *Recuerdos de niñez y de mocedad* begin with unreflective physicality and progress to complex "readings" of the landscape. Unamuno's first mention of his childhood experience of the countryside is the remembrance of his excursions to the fields on the edge of the city with his teacher: "Indecible es el efecto que en nosotros, niños urbanos, nacidos y criados entre calles, causaba el campo. Y gracias que le había, fresco y verde, a los ejidos mismos de la villa. El campo es ante todo para el niño aire y luz libre" (34). Two features of this summary are notable.

Unamuno describes his experience of nature from the very beginning as that of an urban child. Secondly, his initiation into nature occurs on the edge of the city. As in *Paz en la guerra*, the experience of nature occurs in dialogue with the urban experience.

Unamuno describes his first contact with the nature in terms of sheer physical pleasure: light and air and physical freedom. The spiritual dimension of the experience of nature is born with the awakening of adult consciousness, but this unencumbered, direct physical experience is the basis for that future experience. However, Unamuno associates even this experience of uncomplicated physicality with language, recalling how, as soon as they were released, he and his classmates would run immediately to the Nervión River to watch the new steamboats, and how when they saw one they would shout out its name: "¡el Vizcaíno Montañés!, o cual fuese su nombre. Esto de repetir el nombre de una cosa delante de ella es uno de los placeres de la infancia; es como si en cierto modo nos adueñáramos espiritualmente de ella" (35). This infantile pleasure can be extended to a description of the adult writer's landscape writings, especially since the emphasis of these descriptions is not on the exotic, but on a verbal evocation of something familiar to or easily imaginable by the reader.

Unamuno and his classmates' experience of the animal world, especially of insects, is also related to language. Describing the games they played with flies, Unamuno emphasizes nomenclature: sapo, solitaña, zapatero, cochorro (36). From individual names he progresses to the popular rhyme about *solitaña* (36), and from this to a story in his children's reader, *El amigo de los niños*, about a boy who passes his time locked up in a prison hunting flies (37). The succeeding chapter on the *cochorro* follows a similar pattern: 1) taxonomy, both scientific and popular and regional variants: "Llámase en Bilbao cochorro a lo que en otras regiones de España recibe los nombres de jorge, bacallerín, abejorro, sanjuanero, en francés *hanneton*—palabra de origen germánico que vale tanto como "gallito"—y cuyo mote entomológico es *melolontha vulgaris*" (40); 2) schoolboys' slang: "Y nosotros disputábamos sobre quién tenía el cochorro más trabajador, pues a ese revolteo le llamábamos trabajar" (41); 3) popular rhymes: "Y le cantábamos al cachorro para animarle en su tarea: Pavolea, chistolea, vola, vola tú (bis), palabras litúrgicas con unos verbos que sólo en esa fórmula semimágica se empleaban" (42); and 4) a context of classical culture: "Más tarde he sabido que ya Aristóteles nos habla del melolantha como un juguete de los niños griegos, un juguete clásico. Y me he sentido orgulloso al saber el clásico abolengo de uno de los juguetes de mi niñez" (43). This is a good example of the relationship between language and nature in Unamuno's writings.

In chapter 12 about the bully Luis and the power hierarchy among boys, nature is presented once more in terms of sheer physicality. When Guillermo challenges Luis, they meet in an empty field: "una mañana tibia de primavera; había llovido la noche antes y estaba mojado el suelo. A los dos, Luis y Guillermo, les retozaba en el cuerpo la savia [. . .]" (62). The boys are a part of nature, under the influence of the same vital forces that transform the landscape in the springtime. "A Luis y Guillermo el cuerpo, envuelto en primavera, les pedía cachetes" (62). Here physicality seems to erase the boundaries between the youths and their natural environment, and they blend into the landscape, but ultimately this feat is only achieved through language: the "sap" in their bodies, wrapped in a springtime that is given metaphoric materiality.

In the next significant section on landscape, Unamuno connects the experience of the outdoors to both physical and spiritual experience. Unamuno describes how his physical strength languished with the development of his intellect, and how, as a result, he was prescribed a daily walk to the New

Bridge of the Nervión and back: "Mientras el pecho se hincha de aire fresco y libre," one is released from everyday cares and "goza de una pasividad calmosa, en un aplanamiento lleno de vida, el desfilar de las sensaciones fugitivas" (90). In contact with nature, "[e]l pensamiento libre yerra de una cosa en otra, se fija en lo que pasa y pasa con ello, se identifica con lo fugitivo y sueña lo que ve. ¡Qué triste tener que pasar de aquellos paseos al aula oscura!" (91). It is during these repeated, almost ritualistic walks that his imagination is freed up, while physical strength develops. This relationship, between the routine of the walk and the spontaneity of thought, parallels that of chapter 13 on the role of holidays within routine. Motion through landscape encourages the activity of dreaming, not of the exotic, but of what is right in front of one, similar to the action of saying the name of the steamboat that one is simultaneously seeing. Sight is active; it does not merely register one's surroundings but also acts upon it. The activity of the imagination in landscape is contrasted to the environment of the school. Of his study of Latin, which he undertook with such enthusiasm, Unamuno recalls that "Perdí un tiempo hermoso y empecé a consumir la frescura de mi seso" (83). This repetitive exercise contributes to the decline of his physical condition for which his walks were subsequently prescribed, as he is consumed by "una como tristeza prematura acompañada de pobreza física" (84). Summarizing what he learned in his first year of high school, which he completed without distinction, he recalls: "Aprendí algo de latín, los ríos de la China, las montañas de Turquestán, los principados del Danubio y hasta el número de habitantes que veinte años antes habían tenido las principales ciudades del globo" (84). The dry study of Latin is contrasted with the spontaneous language games of the pupils in chapter 8, and the rote geography of names with the direct experiences of the natural world. Nature integrates physical, intellectual and imaginative experience, while the classroom walls separate these dimensions of human experience.

Unamuno integrates the experience of language with that of nature most strikingly in the second half of chapter 3 in which he describes his vacations in his grandmother's country house. Like Ignacio in *Paz en la guerra*, the young Unamuno's experience in the village is that of a city boy, "donde los chicos de la escuela se burlaban de nuestras largas blusas" (91). It is the summers at his grandmother's when "me abrieron el alma al sentimiento de la naturaleza" (91). This statement is immediately followed by a description of a literary experience: "Y no olvidaré el profundo efecto que me causó la lectura allí, por las noches, de la candorosa novela de Trueba, *Mari Santa*, al ver que en el libro se hablaba de lugares que podía yo ver desde el corredor de aquel caserío [. . .]. Entonces empecé a sentir lo que es vivir en un lugar consagrado por el arte" [92]. Like the boys who shouted at the Vizcaíno montañés, literature affects the reader's perception of the reality to which it refers. Trueba's novel is not the only text that influences Unamuno's country summers. Jules Verne provides inspiration for games with paper boats in the canals that form in the orchard when the tide from the estuary is especially high.

But literature does not only inform the experience of nature: nature also influences the experience of literature. The most important statement of the relationship between literature and landscape in *Recuerdos* is Unamuno's description of his first serious experience with literature while at his grandmother's house. Unamuno explains: "Traigo aquí estos recuerdos campesinos porque van unidos muy especialmente a los de mi tercer año de bachillerato, el de retórica." Unamuno recalls how at this time he would climb up into a pear tree in his grandmother's orchard to a make-shift treehouse: "una vez allí, entre las hojas que empezaban a caer—era en los apacibles atardeceres de las postrimerías de octubre—, me ponía a repetir una frase hasta aprendérmela de memoria" (93). He continues:

> Y aburrido pronto de la lección corría hojas y me iba a buscar en los ejemplos aquellos versos de Zorrilla que dicen:
>
> Mi voz fuera más dulce
> que el ruido de las hojas
> mecidas por las auras
> del oloroso abril... (94)

With the repetition of the word *hojas*, Unamuno creates a semantic dialogue between text and environment. One crosses over into the other: the pages of the book, the falling leaves of the pear tree, and the gently rustling leaves in Zorrilla's poem. Unamuno continues this playful mixing: the melody of the verses "hicieron agitarse a las hojas de mi alma mientras se agitaban las hojas del peral [. . .] Y paseándome en la huerta, a la caída de las horas y las hojas, declamaba los versos, yéndoseme los oídos tras ellos" (94). There is a synchronicity between textual and real worlds. Voice connects language with nature, as it is given metaphoric materiality. Also, the density of repetition (of *hojas* with its various meanings) in this passage is an early example of the lyrical element in Unamuno's prose writings on landscape. Finally, the setting of the pear tree as well as the orchard may possibly allude to Saint Augustine, and to the latter's epiphany that connects both text and physical environment.

The verses Miguel reads transform his experience of the environment. Zorrilla speaks of the "desierto / la inmensa soledad" and it is notable that Unamuno does not speak of being imaginatively transported to the desert, but rather of how the idea of the desert superimposes itself on his experience of his immediate surroundings: "Estas palabras me levantaban el alma, imaginándome la inmensa soledad del desierto en aquella risueña y doméstica huerta de parras, maíces, frutales y pájaros" (95). This juxtaposition and telescoping of spaces is something Unamuno plays with in various writings on landscape.

The simplicity of the verses' rhythms also seems to facilitate and experience of integration with the natural environment: "¡Qué hechizo me producirían los versos por sí mismos, por su halago al oído!" (95). Unamuno memorizes the verses, so his attention is not on reading and understanding, but reproducing sounds, which produces a particular pleasure in an open space. The pleasure lies not in metric sophistication but in metric simplicity: "Verdad es que Zorrilla realiza un problema de máximos y mínimos, y es el de dar la menor poesía que puede darse con la mayor armonía rítmica" (95). All of this pleasure is contrasted, as in the case of learning Latin, with the dryness of the subject of rhetoric. The freshness of language is found outdoors. In conclusion, in *Recuerdos de niñez y mocedad*, Unamuno presents his early experiences of nature and of language as integrally related. They are interdependent, with each enriching the other.

In *Las confesiones de un pequeño filósofo* (1904), Azorín also presents literature and landscape as integrally related. The opening segments of the book, in its second edition (1909), are a progression from extra to intradiegetic landscape. In "Dónde escribí este libro," the author says that, for this preface to the new edition, the best thing he can do is to describe the setting where he wrote it. There follows a detailed description of the interior Alicantine geography and of the house where he wrote the book, similar to the descriptive passages that open *La voluntad* and *Antonio Azorín*. The emphasis is on the exemplary characteristics of both countryside—"del campo alicantino castizo" (39)—and the characteristics of the typical Levantine house. The layout of the house is described without detailed description of any particular item of decoration (in contrast to the opening passages of *La voluntad* and *Antonio Azorín*). While Azorín is clearly describing a particular house, the description emphasizes its exemplary over its particular characteristics.

Following the preface in the second edition (opening the book in the first) is a sort of prologue entitled "Orígen de este libro," which refers to how a third-person character, Azorín, is persuaded by his friends to desist in his plans to run for office, and to write an intimate book instead. His gifts, say his friends, lie not in drafting political programs or giving speeches, but in his "palabra [. . .] sencilla y tranquila" (43). This section acts as a barrier between the real world and the fictionalized space of the "memoir." Furthermore, it introduces the question of genre. The final line reiterates that "éste es el libro, lector, que ha escrito *Antonio Azorín*, en lugar de un programa político" (44). The *sui generis* text that follows is thus substitutional, filling the space of another form that it replaces. But in the very title, with its original subheading, two other genres are suggested: the novel and the confession. This flurry of genres at the beginning of the work all carry out a similar function: that of using conventional generic terms to establish a literary space that the anomalous text can occupy, somewhat like the way the pre-established space of a canvas is required for a painting. Finally, Martínez Ruiz places the emphasis on intimate, rather than public, writing.

This first proper chapter of the book is an intradiegetic mirror of the prologue. The narrator of "Yo no sé si escribir" is no longer identical with the biographical author who is assumed (by convention) to speak in the prologue, but an ambiguous "I" that floats between the real author and the character Azorín introduced in the prologue. Similarly, the setting described in chaper 1 is a step removed from the setting of "Dónde escribí este libro" (43). The typical and exemplary is replaced by the specific. What had been identified only as "una casa del campo alicantino castizo" (39) becomes the specific location of

Martínez Ruiz's family property in el Collado de Salinas. While the prologue doesn't mention specific times of day and only alludes to a flowering season, the narrator of chapter 1 evokes time and place with more concrete sensuality: "Es medianoche; el campo reposa en un silencio augusto; cantan los grillos en un coro suave y melódico; las estrellas fulguran en el cielo fuliginoso; de la inmensa llanura de las viñas sube un frescor grata y fragante" (45). The evening has an expansive, mysterious quality. Furthermore, the furnishings of the room where the narrator writes are described—the simple table, and the lamp that casts a soft glow in the darkened room—and most importantly, the books that line the shelves: "Cervantes, Garcilaso, Gracián, Montaigne, Leopardi, Mariana, Vives, Taine, La Fontaine" (45).

Within the body of the memoir, Azorín's first recollection of nature, like Unamuno's, is connected to sheer physical pleasure and to play. In chapter 4, "La alegría," the narrator describes the only game he remembers from his childhood. In this game, each boy stands in a ray of moonlight, challenging the other to dislodge him from his spot. The mere act of play is a novelty in the severe routine of the young José, and has a variant in nocturnal excursions with a neighborhood servant—"la mujer más estupenda que he conocido" (50)—strangely dressed like a witch, who takes the boys to some nearby fields, where "nos revolcábamos, bañados por la luz de la luna, en estas noches serenas de Levante, sobre la blanda y cálida paja" with the woman who "nos regalaba la alegría" (51). In Azorín's memoir, this early experience of nature has an oneiric element as well, which is also associated with the creative process: the genesis of the book is said to have taken place on a summer evening.

The next chapter, "El solitario," presents the flip side of the experience of nature in "La alegría." In "La alegría," nature is a space of physical pleasure, and of connection with other human beings, of both friendship and erotic feeling. "El solitario" describes the employer of the servant who brought the boys to the fields in the moonlight. Even in his urbane life, his sign is nature. This man, "un poco triste, un poco cansado," loves to plant trees and frequents the local casino's garden with his two dogs to feed the birds, all of which he knows and calls "por sus nombres particulares" (53). This solitary man chooses nature over his fellow human beings: "los pájaros, los dos lebreles silenciosos y los árboles eran sus únicos amigos" (53). Soon nature becomes a vehicle for even greater separation from society. Disillusioned with the fickle and ungrateful nature of his fellows, he finally retires to a mountaintop house in the country: "Ya no volvió jamás a pisar el pueblo ni a entrar en comunión con los hombres; llevaba una vida de solitario entre las florestas que él había hecho arraigar y crecer" (52). Nature is a boundary instead of a space of communion. However, he maintains one link to society: the daily papers he has brought to him from town and which are "como una lucecita, como un débil lazo de amor que aun los hombres que más abominan de los hombres conservan [. . .]" (53). The notion of literature as a connector between distinct spaces / landscapes is reinforced by the metaphor of the *lucecita*, a common synechdoche for the train in Azorín's work (ex. "Una lucecita roja" in *Castilla*). Periodical literature, like the train, is a modern invention that connects people and places in a new way. Finally, the *lucecita* in chapter 5 seems to counterbalance the *lunita* of chapter 4. In the latter, moonlight connects individuals in a landscape of play, dream, and eroticism; in the former, literature is a light that connects solitudes.

In other sections Martínez Ruiz describes the early impact of landscape on the development of his imagination. Among the most important is the impression of the landscape visible from the study room at the back of the school, a landscape that the narrator says "ha influido gratamente en mi vida de artista" (63). The "pequeña vega yeclana" recalls Unamuno's fondness for spaces that are "recogidos" (63). In this landscape, the geometrical lines of the cultivated fields and the straight, white highway are contrasted with the undulating curves of the hills, "los azarbes [que] se deslizan culebreando." This landscape is "verde y suave," it extends like a "fresca y clara alfombra." The trees "destacan su nota alegre" and the flatness is "grata" (63). The window intensifies the compositional aspect of the landscape and emphasizes the subjectivity of the viewer.[7] The landscape outside the study window is a welcoming space into which his imagination can expand. It is open yet contained: first, by the frame of the window, and second, by its relative "smallness," that Martínez Ruiz emphasizes in the expressions cited above. The mystery of the familiar landscape receives its fullest expression in the focal point of the composition, another closed or containing space: "una casa pequeña cuyas paredes blancas asoman por lo alto de una floresta cerrada por una verja de madera" (64).

In conclusion, while Unamuno presents a vision of interdependency between language and landscape and the production of meaning in his memoir, in *Confesiones* Martínez Ruiz presents landscape as an essential stimulus for his imagination, and also, to an extent, as analogous to literature: both are spaces of imagination, and both can be connective forces between people and things that may not be objectively connected in reality.

---

[7] To an extent, the siege of Bilbao that Unamuno describes in *Paz en la guerra* has a similar effect upon the city: as the circle around the city intensifies, the life within the walls becomes more intense within this "frame."

Chapter Three

The Intellectual as Orphan

In the previous two sections I examined how Unamuno and Martínez Ruiz develop the persona of the writer-intellectual in the context of two genres: the novel and the memoir. In Unamuno and Azorín's early novels—*Paz en la guerra* and *La voluntad*—the largely autobiographical character of the intellectual emerges from a background, secondary position, to the foreground through the course of the novel. Landscape is a space associated with the solitary experience of the intellectual, and it plays a role in the development of his perspective. At moments, landscape is also a vehicle for the intellectual to construct a relationship to members of lower socio-economic classes, reflecting the desire of turn-of-the-century intellectuals to cultivate a relationship with, and to an extent assume the role of spokesperson for, the laboring classes.

In the memoir, each author creates a narrative of the intellectual's childhood and adolescent development. In both memoirs, the experience of nature is associated with early acts of reading and writing. The environment becomes an element in the process of literary reception. Reading often occurs close to nature: outdoors or near windows with views. In sum, what is presented is a model of reading that does not disconnect the reader from the extratextual world, but which promotes an experience of fluidity between the textual and exterior worlds.

In the previous two chapters, I commented on elements of orphanhood in the various permutations of the intellectual character in Martínez Ruiz and Unamuno's early novels. Their self-characterization as orphans is not surprising given that the writers of the Generation of 1898 in general defined themselves not only by their nonconformity with contemporary cultural and artistic values, but also by their reaction, often openly hostile, against the prior generation. Brooks observes that:

> paternity is a dominant issue within the great tradition of the nineteenth-century novel (extending well into the twentieth century), a principal embodiment of its concern with authority, legitimacy, the conflict of generations, and the transmission of wisdom. (63)

The orphan character has the advantage of having a "choice among possible fathers from whom to inherit, and in the choosing [. . .] he comes to define his own authority." As Hana Wirth-Nesher observes in her study of Dickin's Pip and Twain's Huckleberry Finn, literary orphans "by virtue of their not being limited by the rules and constraints of parents and kin, are free to seek spiritual surrogate parents and moral codes. The rise of the novel is in part a response to the newly found freedom of such individuals in the wake of feudalism" (260). Orphan characters are perhaps especially appealing for writers of this period because their narratives are most apt for conceptualizing conflict with patriarchal authority figures as well as for envisioning a more open-ended future.

The orphan, like the traveler, the poet, and the intellectual, is a persona whose identity is bound up with a notion of solitude, a prevalent theme in Unamuno and Azorin's writings. Furthermore, orphaned characters often have a special relationship with nature. The natural world is a frequently a space that in part substitutes the missing parent.

In this section, in order to provide some context for understanding the implications of Unamuno and Azorín's incorporation of elements of orphanhood in their figuration of intellectual characters, I will briefly examine some earlier representations of orphanhood, in works by Caballero, Galdós, and Clarín, drawing attention to some central features that are relevant to the use of orphanhood as part of authorial self-representation in writings by Azorín and Unamuno.

Clemencia

Clemencia, the orphan protagonist of Fernán Caballero's novel of the same name (1852), is one of the most fully realized female orphan characters in nineteenth-century Spanish fiction. Much of Clemencia's story is directly affected by her orphan status. Her narrative begins when she is taken into her aunt's home after her early education in a convent. There she is a marginal figure to family life. Open and affectionate by nature, Clemencia is converted by her "acogida [. . .] poco cordial" into a "pobre niña, humillada y rechazada," who "lloró y dudó de sí" (92). Her first marriage is in part determined by her dependent status. When Fernando Ladrón de Guevara asks for Clemencia's hand, her aunt readily consents, something she would not have done had it been one of her own daughters.[8] Clemencia bears her

[8] The grouping of the three girls recalls fairy tale structures, in which threes occur with frequency. The orphan figure, in general, seems linked to narratives of hero / heroine struggles that precede realist fiction. In *Clemencia*, the fairytale, or allegorical nature of the narrative is underscored by the names of the three young women: Constancia, Alegría and Clemencia. The motif of the three daughters occurs in Azorín's writings as well, for example, when

situation with a resignation that Caballero characterizes as Christian (140), but Clemencia's patience, resignation and self-sacrifice are also in part a pragmatic psychological response to her dependent, orphan status. Clemencia simply has fewer opportunities for self-determination than do her cousins. Clemencia's peculiar situation affects the evolution of her narrative. Peter Brooks points out the importance of the child-parent relationship to the development of the child's sense of narrative that Roland Barthes observed:

> [T]he child appears to "discover" the Oedipus complex and the capacity for constructing coherent narrative at about the same stage in life. The most fully developed narratives of the child become a man all seem to turn on the uncertainty of fatherhood, to use this uncertainty to unfold the romance of authority vested elsewhere, and to test the individual's claim to personal legitimacy within a struggle of different principles of authority. (64)

Clemencia initially makes no apparent effort to determine her own narrative, in contrast to her cousins, especially Constancia, who plots a romantic narrative for herself. The early part of Clemencia's story contains little action and emphasizes custom, character, iterative action, and perception. The first major narrative event in her life—her marriage to Ladrón de Guevara—is in fact an almost entirely passive one. Summarizing Clemencia's marriage to Ladrón de Guevara, the narrator states that her emphasis has not been so much on the particularities of the events, but rather on the impression they have left, thus resolving action (narrative) into stasis and inwardness (impression): "Si hemos referido con rápida aglomeración todos estos eventos tan importantes en la vida de nuestra protagonista

---

Azorín has a sentimental attachment to Pepita, one of Sarrió's three daughters, in *Antonio Azorín*.

ha sido porque con la misma acaecieron, y que la propia impresión penosa, indefinida y amarga que dejará este relato en la imaginación del lector, fue la sola que dejaron estos sucesos al cabo de algún tiempo en el ánimo de Clemencia" (141).

The development of Clemencia's own narrative coincides with her receipt of the letter from Ladrón de Guevara's parents stating their wish to accept Clemencia as a daughter (145). Before departing for the coast with Constancia, she writes to her in-laws explaining that she will be delayed, "añadiendo que ansiaba por el día feliz en que dejase de ser huérfana, hallando padres en los de su marido" (149). The possibility of surrogate parents initiates a period of narrative activity in Clemencia's life. However, this narrative development is deferred until after Clemencia's trip to the country, a delay that coincides with the hiatus in her movement towards parents.

Clemencia's story, when it finally develops, is distinct from the paradigm of the male struggling with authority figures for legitimacy. Brooks notes a discrepancy between male and female-centered ambition:

> The female plot [. . .] takes a more complicated stance toward ambition, the formation of an inner drive toward the assertion of selfhood in resistance to the overt and violating male plots of ambition, a counter-dynamic which, from the prototype *Clarisa* on to *Jane Eyre* and *To the Lighthouse*, is only superficially passive, and in fact a reinterpretation of the vectors of plot. (39)

Given the relative scarcity of external events in Clemencia's story, it is logical that Caballero should use Clemencia's relationship to her environment as a technique of character development. Clemencia's relationship to her environment is characterized by stillness and reflection more than by purposeful movement. This is most intensely evident in Clemencia's first experience of nature, narrated in chapter 11, when Clemencia accompanies Constancia to the family's country house on the coast, to "cure" the latter of an attachment contrary to her family's wishes. (The pretext Clemencia's aunt devises—that it is Clemencia who is convalescent—ironically becomes truth, as Clemencia begins there to recuperate from her unhappy marriage). The rural environment of the house is presented in the context of a comparison between romantic modes of feeling and living, represented by Constancia, and a Christian-orphan mode of experience, represented by Clemencia. At the center of both their experiences of nature is solitude. The house where the women are staying is adorned with "la imagen de nuestra Señora de la Soledad, de la cual tomaba la posesión su nombre" (150). However, the two young women experience solitude differently. Constancia says, "Yo no temo a la soledad; para mí es todo soledad donde no está él" (153). Constancia's embrace of her forced isolation is romantic and self-aggrandizing. Furthermore, it is self-consciously literary: "¡Si lo que me sucede a mí se pusiese en una novela, se diría que eran dislates de novelistas, que se devanan los sesos para inventar cosas extraordinarias!" (152). Clemencia's experience of nature, in turn, is quite different. Unperturbed by romantic passion, and with a much more humble sense of self, Clemencia feels accompanied by the objects in her environment, in contrast to the isolation that she often experiences in society: "Al contrario de Constancia, que se sentía presa en aquella soledad campestre y tranquila, Clemencia se sentía simpáticamente acompañada por los bellos objetos de la naturaleza. Criada en un convento, nunca había disfrutado del campo, y su alma se ensanchaba al recorrer aquellos campos, al vagar por aquellas playas" (153). Despite these differences, however, Clemencia's mode of experiencing nature is also literary. Describing the delight Clemencia feels on contemplating the sky, Caballero writes, "como dice Lamartine, allí donde el cielo sonríe, impulsa al hombre a sonreír también" (153), and shortly after, "Todo aquello le infundía mil sensaciones y pensamientos, pues como dice Balzac: le paisage a des idées; el paisaje tiene ideas" (154).

Clemencia's experience of nature progresses to a more spiritual register when she imagines how peaceful it would be to die in the midst of such surroundings:

> ¡Oh! ¡cuán dulce sería—se decía Clemencia—, con una conciencia pura y tranquila, acostarse en brazos de esas fragantes yerbas, y los ojos alzados a la brillante bóveda, morir alumbrada por el sol, suavemente arrullado nuestro último sueño por el dulce murmullo de las perezosas olas de verano, y el susurro del aura entre las plantas, subiendo así nuestra alma en un himno de alabanzas y adoración al cielo, como se alza a las alturas la armoniosa alondra! (155)

Death is represented as integration with nature. This vision of death, as the conclusion of life (time and narrative) dissolved into nature (space), inspires some positive feeling. In conclusion, Clemencia's experience in nature both incorporates and also represents a departure from some Romantic attitudes toward nature and solitude. Nature offers the possibility of a sensuous peacefulness and imaginative liberation, but it does not necessarily inspire withdrawal from or rejection of the norms of society.

La Regenta

Ana Ozores loses mother at birth, and is effectively abandoned by her father soon after. She therefore spends much of her childhood alone, and solitude will be an essential characteristic of the adult Ana as well. Mercedes Vidal Tibbits, in her article on the theme of Ana's solitude, distinguishes between voluntary solitude, which "puede ser una experiencia positiva, de reconocimiento de sí mismo y de desarrollo interno," and that other kind which is more often the case, solitude that is "una experiencia dolorosa, que le ha sido impuesta, de la que anhela escapar" (1535); it is this latter kind that afflicts Alas's heroine. While this is certainly true, Ana, like the isolated Clemencia, does experience a more positive form of solitude during the moments when she comes into contact with nature. One sign of the positive quality of these solitary moments in nature—in Loreto as a child and adolescent, and in el Vivero as an adult—is the fact that they are accompanied by her moments of most intense literary-creative production, as Gonzalo Sobejano has studied, and to whose article I will return shortly.

In *La Regenta* as in *Clemencia*, the discovery of nature is linked to convalescence. When the delicate Anita is a small child, "[a]consejaron los médicos aires del campo y del mar para la niña" (76). For this reason, her father, Don Carlos, purchases a country house from a friend in "un pueblecillo pintoresco, puerto de mar y saludable a todos los vientos" (76). There, under the malicious rigidity of her nanny, Doña Camila, Anita daydreams in her room—like the young Ignacio—of "espacios que ella creaba llenos de ensueños confusos, pero iluminados por una luz difusa que centelleaba en su cerebro" (78). Related to her first experiences of literature is her discovery of nature; for Ana, as for Azorín and Unamuno, these experiences are interrelated. Furthermore, it is at this time that she begins a poem that will become a "text" consubstantial with her life: "A los veintisiete años Ana Ozores hubiera podido contar aquel poema desde el principio al fin, y eso que en cada nueva edad le había añadido una parte" (78). This "subtext" of Ana's life parallels, and in some ways competes with, her exterior life narrative. Gonzalo Sobejano writes: "Ana Ozores fue primeramente—y a través de su historia siguió siéndolo en cuanto pudo— poeta. El «misticismo»y la «pasión» (no digamos la «familia») resultan al fin transformaciones o sustituciones de su vocación primaria: la poesía" (1986, 223). This fact is important not only to an understanding of the character of Ana Ozores; it is an example of interest in artistic vocation or process in itself, not just in the artistic result. This theme occurs in various writings by Clarín (In "Las dos cajas," for example) and is frequent in the Generation of '98. In *Paz en la guerra*, Unamuno shows Pachico at work writing a text that cannot satisfactorily express his feelings about Ignacio's death. Sobejano describes elements of Ana's experience that correspond to ideas of inspiration (Sobejano, *La inspiración de Ana Ozores* 225-226). Pachico also has experiences associated with inspiration, although he does not produce a text. Pachico is never identified specifically as a writer or intellectual, yet he displays traits of both. What seems important to Unamuno is the possession of a vital attitude or vision of life that can have various forms of expression and possibly even no public expression at all. The notion of a distance between an artistic disposition and artistic production is an important theme in both Azorín and Unamuno's writings, to which I will return in the following chapter.

With respect to Ana's literary development, Sobejano observes that the moments in which Ana's poetic activities are most extensively described—in Loreto, as both a child of six and a teenager, and later as an adult in el Vivero—both feature experiences of nature. Furthermore, I would emphasize the fact that her impulse to write is motivated in each case by a sense of lack, or need, which is explicitly associated with her orphan status. The first part of the poem that the infantile Anita begins in Loreto is "compuesto de las lágrimas de sus tristezas de huérfana maltratada y de fragmentos de cuentos que oía a los criados y a los pastores de Loreto" (78). Her excursions into nature inspire her to poetic composition: "Siempre que podía se escapaba de casa; corría sola por los prados, entraba en las cabañas, donde la conocián y acariciaban, sobre todo los perros grandes; solía comer con los pastores. Como Poussin cogía hierbas en los prados para estudiar la naturaleza que trasladaba al lienzo, Anita volvía de sus escapatorias de salvaje con los ojos y la fantasía llenos de tesoros que fueron lo mejor que gozó en su vida" (78). The interruption of Ana's exploration of nature at this point is in part caused by Doña Camila's association of nature with vice. Regarding Ana's moonlight escapade with Germán she says: "¡Si ya lo decía yo! El instinto..., la sangre... No basta la educación contra la naturaleza" (80).

Later, as a teenager, orphanhood and nature are again associated in her almost mystical experience that begins with her discovery of St. Augustine and culminates in the verses she composes to the Virgin Mary in the pine grove. At this point Ana's aesthetic sense has moved beyond the epics of her childhood. Sobejano observes that her literary experience in the pine grove has elements of the sublime. It takes place in "un escenario natural que ofrece todos los caracteres de lo sublime: grandeza y poder ilimitados, de apariencia sobrehumana, que elevan el deleite de la hermosura a un grado álgido de asombro" (*La inspiración de Ana Ozores* 225).

In this chapter Clarín represents Ana's orphanhood, her attraction to literature, and nature, as being interrelated. Reading St. Augustine's *Confessions*,[9] "lloró [. . .], como sobre el seno de una madre." Ana seeks both in literature and nature what she lacks in real life—a mother—and the fact that she writes her verses to the Virgin is revealing about the meaning that literature has for her. The question that she asks herself just before she enters into a state of inspiration—"¿Aquel vacío de su corazón iba a llenarse?" (87)—could refer as well to the absence of her mother, and the resounding "yes" that she experiences in

[9] In *Paz en la guerra*, when Pachico's faith vacilates and his uncle begs him to go to confession, the local priest exhorts him "contra la lectura en general y recomendándole vida de distracción y campo, y las *Confesiones* de San Agustín [. . .]" (197).

response again suggests the idea that literature, in this case the creation of literature, responds to a lack.

Ana's second principal experience of nature occurs in chapter 27 when she travels with her husband to el Vivero. Once again, it is a trip to the country motivated by illness, although this time Ana's convalescence is more spiritual and psychological. Ana resembles Constancia here, as she has also been afflicted by her own Romantic vision of life. However, in her recovery she more nearly resembles Clemencia, as here nature is associated not with exalted spiritual states, but with harmony, humility, and the possibility of peace. However, the fact that this promise proves ultimately illusory connects *La Regenta* more firmly with the succeeding novels of Unamuno and Azorín, in which nature is experienced at intervals, its promise never permanently fulfilled.

Ana's visit to el Vivero is also connected with a fertile period of diary writing, as Sobejano has analyzed (*La inspiración de Ana Ozores* 226-229). The journal, of which we see fragments in this chapter, resembles Antonio Azorín's diary in part III of *La voluntad*. Like Ana, Antonio Azorín is a writer, but one who in the end is defined not by his public writing—his articles for the local press and his failed experiments as a journalist in Madrid—but by intimate texts not meant for public consumption. Similarly, in *Antonio Azorín* the protagonist's literary expression blossoms in his letters to Pepita, once again a private document meant only for one reader, and the style of these letters persists in the descriptive fragments later in the book (and continue in the travel writings), suggesting that these originate in a conception of intimate rather than public writing. Furthermore, Ana's literary experience in the countryside of el Vivero leads her, like Pedro Antonio in *Paz en la guerra*, to reconnect with her childhood, a connection expressed by the text she has been elaborating since her first adventures outdoors in

Loreto. In summary, in *La Regenta* the themes of nature, orphanhood, and literature are interconnected.

Ana is never able to resolve her orphan situation. Her husband, Victor, is something of a father figure, but their relationship makes his surrogate paternity complicated, and he is also unable to understand her spiritually or intellectually. Her one intellectual and spiritual equal, her confessor, Fermín, ultimately cannot be her surrogate father because he has fallen in love with her. She has no female friend or confidante, and the solace that she might have found in her own experience as a mother is denied to her in her sterile marriage. The unsatisfactory choices offered to Ana with respect to her longing to end her orphanhood, are unsatisfactory because the provincial society to which she belongs is unsatisfactory. Her husband is a limited, unimaginative although well meaning functionary. Fermín is an ambitious man whose economic situation only provided for a clerical career as an outlet for this ambition. Álvaro, her adulterous love interest, is a second-rate, cynical Don Juan. The pettiness and envy of the women in her circle, as well as her own sense of class difference, prevent her from forming female friendships or finding a maternal surrogate. Clarín uses the emotional dynamics of the orphan plot, consistently frustrating its successful resolution, to highlight the deficiencies of Ana's society.

Miau

While Luisito Cadalso is not the ostensible protagonist of Pérez Galdós's *Miau* (1888), the novel opens and nearly closes with this orphaned character. Chapter 1 begins with the rowdy scene of Luisito's school letting out for the day, and his ultimate delivery to surrogate parents initiates the concluding episode of the novel, Villaamil's suicide. Near the end of the final chapter, Villaamil thinks about his grandson and, in a curious gesture, commends himself to "Dios y a San Luisito Cadalso, mi adorado santín" (390). Luisito is afflicted by visions of a heavenly father with whom he converses, and dreams of being a priest.[10] The fact that his visions are of a father (rather than the absent mother), and that he dreams himself of being a father in the clerical sense is curious, as Cadalsito's father provides at least a (literally) nominal presence in his life. However, there is a tension about Luisito's name right from the beginning of the novel. The first name we hear is the taunting one of *Miau* applied by his classmates. Immediately after, the narrator explains that "[e]l pobre chico de este modo burlado se llamaba Luisito Cadalso" (62). The issue of naming is significant to an orphan plot, as Peter Brooks has observed in his analysis of Dickens' *Great Expectations*. This novel, perhaps the most famous nineteenth-century European orphan narrative, begins with the issue of Pip's relationship to his name.

> Pip when we first see him is himself in search of the "authority"—the word stands in the second paragraph of the novel—that would define and justify—authorize—the plot of his ensuing life.
>
> The "authority" to which Pip refers here is that of the tombstone which bears the names of his dead parents, the names that have already been displaced, condensed, and superceded in the first paragraph, where Pip describes how his "infant tongue" (literally, a speechless tongue: a catachresis that points to a moment of emergence, of entry into language) could only make of the name, Phillip Pirrip, left to him by his dead parents, the monosyllabic Pip. [. . .] This originating moment of Pip's narration and his narrative

[10] Luisito displays an intensely vivid imagination and spiritual vocation that liken him to Ana Ozores. These characteristics, which could be signs of a poetic-artistic temperament, are, like the same qualities in Ana Ozores, linked to the orphan's lack. In Luisito's case the motivating lack is that of a real father.

is a self-naming that already subverts whatever authority could be found in the text of the tombstones. (115)

A similar phenomenon occurs at the opening of *Miau.* Luisito is referred to initially by the derogatory nickname of the female members of his household—Miau is effectively a matronym—but also a non-name, like Pip, childish and onomatopoeic. His legal name is only revealed afterwards, and it is undermined by his nickname, similar to the way the name of the protagonist of *Great Expectations* is undermined by that of "Pip." Luisito's visions of god and his vocational inclinations clearly have something to do with the inadequacy of his biological father, which becomes apparent through the novel, and culminates in Victor's final willingness to part with his son in exchange for forgiveness of a debt.

The issue of naming is reinforced by the book's title. The title could indicate that Luisito is in fact the subject of the book, like *Clemencia* or *La Regenta.* Luisito's story defines the extension of the text as almost as fully as Villamil's tragicomic bureaucratic odyssey. The close identity between these two orphan characters is reinforced by the fact that Villaamil's story concludes so shortly after Cadalsito's.

While Luisito's narrative is secondary to the novel, it illuminates the fact that Villaamil's story is also, although less obviously, one of orphanhood: he is first involuntarily orphaned by the State, and later voluntarily orphaned when he severs ties with his family. Villaamil is also an agent of Luisito's orphanhood, which he considers beneficial for the child. While Luisito's future as an orphan is uncertain, it allows for more possibilities than he would have living in his grandmother's house.

Villaamil's self-created orphanhood is also an act of liberation, but he is not permitted a second act of life, only a brief final chapter. In delivering over Luisito, an act that initiates his willful detachment from all his family, Villaamil effectively orphans himself, and this self-orphanhood provokes a feeling of relief and liberation, which he reflects upon over his last supper in a simple tavern:

> Da gusto—pensaba, emprendiéndola resueltamente con el guisote—encontrarse así, tan libre, sin compromiso, sin cuidarse de la familia... porque en buena hora lo diga, ya no tengo familia; estoy solo en el mundo, solo y dueño de mis acciones... ¡Qué gusto, qué placer tan grande! El esclavo ha roto sus cadenas [. . .]." (371)

But Villaamil is not only an orphan of his family; he is an orphan of the State, which he likens to a family: "El Municipio —decía—es hijo de la Diputación Provincial y nieto muy gorrino del Estado, y bien se puede, sin escrúpulo de conciencia, hacer daño a toda la parentela maldita. Tales padres, tales hijos" (380). Villaamil, ejected from the system, has become a figurative orphan of the State. It is when he accepts this rejection, and in turn rejects the State-family, that his status changes from victim to self-determining agent, even if he only uses this self-determination to elect suicide. One thing that is important here is that in the two orphan narratives that Galdós weaves subtly together in *Miau*, the author brings an explicitly public, ideological dimension to the orphan narrative.

Villaamil's self-orphanhood also initiates his contact with nature for the first time in the novel, as he is drawn to the periphery of the city. Chapter 42 opens with a description of the edge of the city at Príncipe Pío. Although this description still includes a few anthropomorphical expressions, which separate Galdós from the younger writers of '98—"un sol picón y alegre," "somnolencia invernal"— the rest of the passage is not unworthy of comparison to a passage by Azorín or Baroja in its specificity of language and objectivity. For example: "apenas verdegueaban los plátanos, las soforas [sic], gleditchas y demás leguminosas estaban completamente desnudas" (370). Galdós's enumeration of very specific names here recalls Azorín. This later description of the Guadarrama observed from the city, and compared with a work of art, also resembles similar descriptions by Azorín and Baroja: "dio la vuelta al cuartel, hasta divisar la sierra, de nítido azul con claros de nieve, como mancha de acuarela extendida sobre el papel por la difusión natural de la gota, obra de la casualidad más que de los pinceles del artista" (370).

What brings Villaamil into contact with nature, in its semi-urban state, is his liberation from family and from the State. Villaamil meditates on how his previous obsessions with work and family did not let him see nature around him: "Paréceme que lo veo por primera vez en mi vida, o que en este momento se acaban de crear esta sierra, estos árboles y este cielo. Verdad que en mi perra existencia llena de trabajos y preocupaciones no he tenido tiempo de mirar para arriba ni para enfrente. Siempre con los ojos hacia abajo" (371). His comment that it seems like the landscape is created by his gaze resembles in general terms an attitude held by Unamuno and Azorín. However, Villaamil is neither an artist nor an intellectual. Villaamil's landscape is intimate.

Of course, it is not anything new that contemplating nature is an activity that belongs to moments of rest. But there is, I think, a difference here. Villaamil's "initiation" (not unlike Pachico's) occurs not far from the city but on its periphery, and implies a changed relationship to that urban space: an undermining of the latter's domination of the individual's life, especially in terms of its ability to define the meaning of the individual's life. That is, nature—even this liminal, semi-urban nature—is a space of critical perspective and alternative values that can be assimilated without permanent retirement from the city.

But Villaamil's odyssey on the edge of the city is tragically short. He is not just out for a walk. His real motivation is to select a place to die. Like Clemencia's meditation on death in her bucolic surroundings, Villaamil's experience of nature is also associated with the idea of death, and the desire for life's narrative to come to an end in a natural setting.[11]

The orphaned self in Unamuno and Azorín
La voluntad

In *La voluntad*, Antonio Azorín's family is virtually omitted. In part I, he lives in apparent solitude in Yecla. When, in part 3, he returns to his family home in Monóvar, the neglected condition of the unoccupied house implies that his parents are no longer alive. As Roberta Johnson has observed, Azorín appears to be a character without a past. While the absence of family serves to accentuate Azorín's general state of isolation from the society around him, his apparent orphanhood has several other consequences.

---

[11] It may be a coincidence, but both Clemencia and Villaamil meditate upon the existence of birds. In *Clemencia*, the birds seem to be a Christian metaphor:

> Los pajaritos cantaban tan alegres en aquella Tebaida, que demostraban en eso cuán poco pertenecían a la tierra.
> —¿Qué admirable poder—se decía Clemencia siguiendo con la vista sus ligeros revoloteos— puso el canto en estos pequeños, lindos e inofensivos seres, que no puede nadie contemplar sin enternecida y tierna simpatía? (153)

In *Miau*, Villaamil sees the birds as free, also, but not from human suffering and sin, but simply from the physical preoccupations of human existence: "Ser pájaro sí que es cómodo y barato. Mírenlos, mírenlos tan campantes, pillando lo que encuentran y zampándoselo tan ricamente [. . .]" (375).

First, the lack of information about Azorín's parents prohibits any possible interpretation of his problems as the result of hereditary factors. Thus, Martínez Ruiz distances *La voluntad* from the naturalist novel. In this respect, Martínez Ruiz's novel is different from Baroja's *Camino de perfección* (1902), a novel with which *La voluntad* is in other ways closely related.[12] In Baroja's novel, there is the suggestion that Fernando Ossorio's problems may be related to a family history of mental instability. Martínez Ruiz also thematizes ideas of biological determinism, as, for example, when he speculates about the Oriental ancestors of the Yeclans in the prologue and part 1, chapter 16; when he calls the Spanish "esta pobre raza paralítica" (215); or through the words of Olaiz (Baroja) in part 2, chapter 8. However, in general Martínez Ruiz seems more preoccupied with spiritual inheritance. This is clear in the description of the sixteenth-century painting "Dama y niña," by the painter Ana Van Cronenburch, in part 1, chapter 2, in which no reference is made to the striking physical resemblance between mother and daughter. Rather, the emphasis is on their spiritual resemblance. "[L]a niña y la anciana, atentas, cuidadosas, reflexivas, parecen escrutar con su mirada interrogante el misterio infinito" (71). Finally, while Antonio Azorín's character is presented as having been shaped by factors of culture, environment, and race, the difference is that they influence him in a general and unmediated way. Azorín seems, almost literally, to be a child of his time. As Martínez Ruiz summarizes at the end of part 2: "Azorín es casi un símbolo; sus perplejidades, sus ansias, sus desconsuelos bien pueden representar toda una generación sin voluntad" (255). By subtracting Azorín's familial history, Martínez Ruiz makes him a less individualized and more exemplary character.

---

[12] Roberta Johnson has studied the relationship between the two novels in detail.

Azorín's figurative orphanhood also gives him a vulnerable side, somewhat less obvious because eclipsed by his pride in being an outsider, a "raro" in the spirit of Baudelaire or D'Annunzio. Despite this apparent indifference to his isolation, Azorín is a character with a fundamental lack: of parenthood, of family, and hence of part of his identity. According to Martínez Cachero, the only real novelistic content of part 1 is Azorín's romantic relationship with Justine. To this I would add that this romance takes on a shade of urgency due to Azorín's orphaned status. He is seeking to remedy a fundamental lack in his life by creating a new bond. The absence of family also gives greater weight to Azorín's relationship with Yuste, who is a surrogate father. Yuste's insufficiency as a mentor is less than his inadequacy as surrogate father. While Azorín's orphan status gives him greater freedom—to determine his own destiny, to distribute his affective relationships in a pattern outside conventional norms—he remains in a state of fundamental lack.

Antonio Azorín

The narrative movement of *Antonio Azorín* begins with Azorín's letters from his dying uncle. As I have suggested in the first chapter of this study, this part of the plot of *Antonio Azorín* resembles that of *Peñas arriba*. Pereda's novel revolves around a question of dynastic succession, in which the nephew of the patriarch is transformed into son and heir. Continuity is secured. In *Antonio Azorín* there is a similar plot, but in a collapsed time period and in a way that undermines the authoritarian structure of patriarchy and inheritance. Azorín's uncle is already enfeebled when the former arrives at his house. The "inheritance" is one of affection, of historical experience and some spiritual values, a legacy of dubious value in the current times. The father-son, intergenerational struggle of *La voluntad*'s orphan plot is substituted by a "weaker" version of an authority struggle. Azorín also experiences true friendship—with Sarrió—and a sentimental attachment to Pepita that seems more positive and energizing (as an impulse to observation and literary expression) than the first Azorín's attachments to Justina or Iluminada. The orphan narrative moves out of the search for parents and the legitimacy that these confer, as Brooks describes, to a search for alternate models of relatedness to fill this lack, that allow for more personal freedom and expression. The orphan's lack (literal or figurative) generates a vacuum that needs to be filled narratively; in *Antonio Azorín,* Martínez Ruiz explores alternative ways to fill that vacuum, privileging models of social relatedness based more on horizontal and diagonal relationships (friendship, uncle-nephew relationship) than vertical ones (father-son, teacher-pupil).

Las confesiones de un pequeño filósofo

One of the most curious features of this book, which is often taken to be only the most scantily disguised memoir, is the fact that the narrator relates the deaths of both parents, although the author's parents were still living when he wrote it.[13] Chapter 44, "Curiosidad y candor," describes the narrator's mother's custom of maintaining notebooks in which she recorded all family events in "su letra grande y fina" (132-133), and her love for the countryside. The title of the chapter suggests that what is most important is an attitude the narrator has inherited from his mother.[14] Chapter 45, "Mi padre," and is a brief portrait like the

---

[13] José Martínez Ruiz's father, Don Isidro Martínez Soriano, died October 30 1919. (García Mercadal 9). His mother, Doña María Luisa Ruiz Maestre, died October 13 1916 (García Mercadal 146).

[14] J. García Mercadal writes:

> Hay, pues, en Azorín, un predominio materno del que dimanan todos los efectos de la personalidad; método de vivir, claridad descriptiva, escrupulosidad, estilo breve, transparente, pensamiento concreto, sin

many others of teachers and relatives in the book. The lack of symmetry between these two titles of consecutive chapters is curious. The chapter describing his mother is titled by the vital attitudes he associates with her, and which he could share. The title "Mi padre" emphasizes the separateness of this figure.

It is surprising how little commentary these two "false obituaries" have elicited. If orphanhood was implicit in the previous two novels, here Martínez Ruiz figuratively and explicitly orphans himself. The two portraits of his parents could certainly have been written without making them obituaries. Furthermore, the kind of death he ascribes to each parent is curious. His mother's death was "larga y terrible" (134); his father's, on the other hand, begins with a simple cold that initiates a process of gradual but inexorable extinguishing of life. Perhaps it is an exaggeration, but it seems that the death he chooses for his mother is a "masculine" death, and that of his father, a "feminine" one. His mother's long and terrible death resembles that of Uncle Verdú described in detail in *Antonio Azorín*. The father, despite his independence and stoicism, in his fear of death resembles the old woman whose death is described in chapter 9 of *Antonio Azorín*. And his death resembles strikingly the kind of death described in the chapter immediately before in the same novel: "Y la muerte está continuamente ante la vista de estos seres. Un día, una de estas mujeres se siente un poco enferma; suspira; implora al Señor; todos los que la rodean suspiran e imploran también" (80). While the narrator's father's reaction is more stoic than that of these women, the type of gradual expiration that he experiences evokes this previous

---

hojarasca... Y de la expresión delicada y el efluvio de ternura en el efecto de la madre, de maneras finas, elegantes y cariñosas, nace un fondo de melancolía, de nostalgia del tiempo ya ido, del concepto de la eternidad. Es decir, una sensibilidad capaz de percibir lo más sutil de la espiritualidad. (13-14)

passage. Without making too much of this detail, it seems that Martínez Ruiz, in the kinds of deaths he ascribes to his fictitious parents, indirectly reverses their gender, and thereby attributes greater power and authority to his mother.

By presenting himself as a de facto orphan, Martínez Ruiz claims for himself the independence, self-determination and open future that are characteristics of orphanhood, as well as the needful stance of the orphan, as part of his persona's sentimental make-up and motivation.

Paz en la guerra

Pachico is the central orphan character in *Paz en la guerra*, though Pedro Antonio also experiences a form of orphanhood when he loses his son. As a counter-figure, Ignacio is a character whose narrative is overdetermined by paternity. Thus, the three central figures of the novel each express something about notions of paternity and orphanhood.

One consequence of Pachico's loss of his parents is his intellectual independence. Pachico has no parent to bind him either to the nationalist or Carlist forces. His uncle, more involved with his interior spiritual life, does not seem to have any particular allegiance: "¿Qué se le daba a él del tan disputado gobierno del mundo?" (440). His only concern is to remove Pachico from Bilbao during the siege. This leaves Pachico much more leeway to judge the war for himself, in contrast to Ignacio, who only in the last moments of his life is permitted this freedom. Furthermore, Pachico's uncle does not assume much authority towards his nephew. When Pachico's faith wavers, his uncle limits himself to begging him to go to confession. And later on, when older and younger man live together but in respectful solitude from one another, Don Joaquín ceases to be concerned about his nephew: "Por lo que hacía a su sobrino, no le preocupaban ya las identidades de éste, puesto que seguía

Pachico, a pesar de ellas, siendo el mismo" (442). The relative detachment of Don Joaquín can be contrasted to the interventions of Ignacio's uncle Pascual in his nephew's education, especially during the vicissitudes of his adolescence: "[T]omó el tío Pascual a su sobrino de su cuenta [. . .]. Queríale cuanto él podía querer según la carne, pero sobre todo se empeñaba en formar sus ideas, considerándole como materia de educación" (170). The degree of freedom that Pachico and Ignacio each have to interpret the world around them and to determine their own lives is inversely proportionate to their subjection to familial authority. Orphanhood is presented as a condition of relative freedom, above all intellectual freedom.

Ignacio does gain a certain perspective towards the abrupt end of his life, and begins to question the meaning of the war and his participation in it. Unamuno suggests that the soldiers who die in battle are, in a way, quasi-orphans. In the scene describing a mass burial of soldiers killed in battle, Unamuno notes that they died "sin el último beso de sus madres" (421) and that furthermore, the graves of those who died "lejos de sus padres" would not even be remembered with a "simple cruz que recordara al caminante de la vida los que regaron con su sangre los campos aquellos de hierro" (422). In a certain way, these soldiers face in death the same situation that Brooks describes Pip facing at the beginning of *Great Expectations*: in their anonymous tombs, they are deprived of their names, and are thus, in a way, orphaned in death.

Finally, there is Pedro Antonio, the "orphaned" father of his only son. It is only after Ignacio's death that the father is able to think critically about the Carlist conflict. After the war's conclusion and his return to Bilbao, he ascends to the top of Begoña and looks out over the villa, meditating: "Allí duerme para siempre, muerto… muerto, ¿por qué? ¡Por la causa! ¿Por la causa? ¿Y por qué causa?" (504). As in *Miau*, an experience of orphanhood, as well as contact with nature on the periphery of the city, initiates a liberation of perspective. He furthermore has a similar revelation to that which Pachico has on the mountaintop, although his experience is one more of feeling than intellect (505).

Orphanhood among the characters gives a specific charge to the feminized landscape, which responds to a need and an absence. The longing is also on the part of the author. Blanco Aguinaga has signaled the importance of the maternal in the development of Unamuno's personality and his concept of landscape: "de la madre a la madre tierra: he aquí el trayecto del niño hombre" (Blanco Aguinaga 1975, 166).[15] The theme of orphanhood has a direct relationship to nature, which offers a form of possible consolation for the orphan's lack.

Nuevo mundo

Although *Nuevo mundo* does not feature descriptions of nature to the same extent as *Paz en la guerra* or even *Recuerdos de niñez y de mocedad*, I will discuss it briefly here because of the presence of the orphanhood theme and its chronological closeness to *Paz en la guerra*. Laureano Robles describes *Nuevo mundo* as "la otra cara de *Paz en la guerra* y el anticipo de

---

[15] José M. López-Marrón takes a Jungian approach in his study of Unamuno's struggle for individuation, and discusses his relationship to both parents. In his writings is a tension between the desire to return to the Great Mother Earth, and simulaneously "la lucha por no ser absorbido por la Madre Terrible y vencer al Padre, que no le permite tomar posesión de la realidad del tiempo y del lenguaje; por otro lado, el personaje lucha entre el logos masculino de su ego consciente y la materia femenina de la inconsciencia que clama ser admitida por el héroe" (ix).

Diario íntimo.[16] However, while *Nuevo mundo* may resemble an autobiography, the protagonist loses both parents, whereas Unamuno's mother was still alive at the time of its composition.[17] Even prior to these deaths, Eugenio, far from home in Madrid, feels distress over the loss of spiritual parents. A figure of the Virgin from his home is recalled repeatedly. At one moment, assailed by spiritual confusion and doubts, he appeals to the Virgen, as he used to do as a child, and it seems to him that the household icon "miraba marchar al hijo pródigo" (51). Immediately afterwards, he loses his spiritual father, the parish priest from his home town who urged him simply to be good: "Cuando supo la noticia de la muerte del anciano párroco, del que dio la última mano a su educación primera, parecióle que se hundía uno de los lazos de sus creencias antiguas con la tierra" (51). This news has barely settled when Eugenio is called home for his mother's death. This loss is followed almost immediately by the loss of his father, when Eugenio is just completing his studies (53). These three deaths recounted within three pages of *Nuevo mundo* seem to exaggerate the impression of Eugenio's orphanhood. His orphanhood radicalizes the solitude he was already suffering in the capital. One night shortly thereafter he experiences a profound sense of disorientation, in which he "se sintió solo, enteramente solo, solo y vacío" (53), and he once again is moved to the rote phrase of supplication of his childhood: "¡Madre de misericordia, favorecedme!" (53).

---

[16] Robles writes that "[a]mbas obras se gestaron casi a la vez; en ocasiones al mismo tiempo" (10). He shows that it must have been completed by March 1896 (11).

[17] Unamuno's father, Don Félix de Unamuno, died in 1870, when Unamuno was six years old (Salcedo 24). Unamuno's mother, Doña Salomé de Jugo, died in 1908.

The theme of the loss of parents, and the longing for spiritual parents, is striking in this novella. Although its is clearly a coincidence that Azorín, in his early semi-autobiography, also alludes to the deaths of his narrator's parents, I believe that it supports the idea of a more general interest in the theme of orphanhood as a form of both solitude and independence in both writers. Eugenio is an individualist who leaves a body of original writings. It would seem that the New World belongs to orphans: those who have been radically severed, or have intentionally separated themselves (like the prodigal son to whom Eugenio refers, who is a sort of temporary orphan) from the most basic ties of society. Families and nations can fall into decadence. Orphans face perils, but their narrative paths are also more open-ended.

Recuerdos de niñez y de mocedad

Both in his generic designation in the title and by using the first person, Unamuno makes this work much more explicitly autobiographical than *Nuevo mundo*. It is curious that in *Recuerdos*, the author's parents are virtually invisible, particularly since parents and/or the idea of parenthood figure prominently in so many of his writings. It would seem that Unamuno subtracts family life as a factor in his formation, while emphasizing solitary experience (reading, walking, meditating, traveling) and group experiences (mainly with childhood schoolmates). Unamuno converts his early life story into one of apparent solitude. Like Azorín, although less explicitly so, in both early versions of his autobiography, *Nuevo mundo* and *Recuerdos*, Unamuno converts himself into a figurative orphan.

In summary, both Azorín and Unamuno incorporate elements of orphanhood in their self-presentation in their early novels and memoirs. Orphanhood was already a subject of interest among Spanish writers from the mid-nineteenth century.

In Caballero and Clarín, the emotional dimension of orphanhood is linked to the experience of nature and landscape. In the writings of Galdós the orphan narrative is given greater historic and ideological content.

The writers of the Generation of 1898—the first generation in which the Spanish word *intelectual* was used as noun that reflected a new cultural phenomenon (Fox, *Ideología* 18)—defined themselves not only by their nonconformity with contemporary cultural and artistic values, but also by their reaction, often openly hostile, against the prior generation. The Generation of 1898 was in many ways a generation of self-styled orphans. The prevalence of orphan characters in their writings is at least partly explained by the orphan narrative's aptness for expressing the desire for change and for a new and different future, as well as anxiety about the same.

Chapter Four

The Artist-Intellectual on the Road

Los pueblos: Towards a national prose poetry

In *Los pueblos* the tendencies that appear in *Confesiones*, especially at the end, are consolidated. What I hope to show in this section is that although the subject matter of *Los pueblos* departs from the more explicitly autobiographical character of the Azorín saga, it is linked to these books by its elements of self-representation. The author is no longer concerned so much with his personal history here, but his preoccupation with his continually evolving literary identity and self-projection before his readers is still evident. In *Los pueblos* he presents himself in transition from writer-intellectual to poet-intellectual. The self-referential content of these pieces is evident in those passages in which the author appears directly as a character, but also in the third-person narratives where the author is only present as narrator. A number of the characters featured in these vignettes permit, and encourage, identification with aspects of the author. The autobiographical project is as important an element in this book as the the search for the authentic nation through direct observation and description of its provincial towns and cities. Or rather, the two projects are inseparable.

The desire for recognition and identity is also a function of the essentially orphaned status of the writer. His is that of a radical solitary, and his social identity needs to be affirmed repeatedly and in each new circumstance. The fact that this is the first book to be signed Azorín is significant. By choosing the patronym of his fictional self, Azorín complicates the process of social identification. That is, his identity cannot be confirmed by any paternal relationship and can only be insisted upon and willed into existence by the solitary writer. Only by constantly writing himself can his identity be sustained. Thus the act of recounting his travels has an existential motive. The writer depends upon his reader in the extra-literary relationship, as he depends upon the people he encounters within the textual reality, for affirmation. This dependence of writer upon reader is more explicit than in previous literature, and is connected to the conditions of literary production and success to which the character Azorín alludes in *La voluntad*, when he speaks about the ephemerality of the contemporary writer's career. The writer is an orphan who depends upon the reader to find his place.

Insofar as it is self-referential and autobiographical *Los pueblos* is, thematically, an extension of the Azorín saga. With respect to the treatment of landscape, *Los pueblos* is somewhat different from the previous books. The descriptions are characterized by greater simplicity of style, a trend already visible in the latter half of *Antonio Azorín* and in *Las confesiones*. What Azorín achieves in *Los pueblos* is the creation of a sense of the landscape as presence, which contrasts with the fleeting or fluid quality of its human inhabitants, by featuring numerous anecdotes that emphasize the fragility of human life and/or identity, and alternating these with sensually vivid landscapes. This poetic enterprise continues a trend in the latter half of *Confesiones* which, Sobejano observes, is "presentánea," as opposed to the first half, which is "sucesiva," and in this emphasis resembles Baudelaire's *Pequeños poemas en prosa* (*Baudelaire* 498).

With respect to form *Los pueblos* consolidates the formal transition from novel to prose poem, fully begun in *Confesiones*, as Gonzalo Sobejano has studied. Unlike *La ruta de Don Quijote*, *Los pueblos* is not determined by a specific travel agenda, and its cohesiveness appears to be based in the relative homogeneity of the pieces. With reference to such pieces both by Azorín and by Unamuno and other contemporaries, which were first published as individual articles and later collected, Martínez Cachero writes: "Como se trata de trabajos bastante unitarios—la unidad viene impuesta por el género «viajes», o el lugar por donde se viaja: una comarca con límites bien definidos, o por alguna otra característica destacada como las escuelas (Bello) o los balnearios (Azorín) en cuanto a paisajes preferiblemente atendidos—, no puede extrañar su fácil integración en un libro" (27). However, what I hope to show is that *Los pueblos* has a deeper coherence that rests upon two factors: first, and principally, the concern with self-presentation that underlies most of the pieces, and which is reinforced by the arrangement of the pieces and recurring elements, and secondly, its character as an aesthetic project. In *Los pueblos*, Azorín deepens his skills in the genre he began using in *Confesiones*: the prose poem. Sobejano has shown the undeniable influence of and inspiration by Baudelaire, especially his *Petits poèmes en prose*, in *Confesiones*. There is, furthermore, greater structural coherence between the pieces that make up *Los pueblos*. As Sobejano notes, vignettes XXIV to XXXVI in *Confesiones* break with the temporal sequence observed up to that point, and that they are "una galería de presencias, simultáneas a lo narrado, sin hilo o continuidad" (*Baudelaire* 498). In *Los pueblos* there is a greater structural coherence between the pieces that goes beyond the successive chronology of the journey.

Beyond the formal coherence of the book, the poetic quality rests in part on the contrast between the presence of the landscape and the absence, or fragility, of the human figures who inhabit or inhabited it. Sometimes this tendency crosses over into a more fantastic vision of landscape, which becomes a space that permits transcendence of the limits of time, space, and personal identity, as in "La novia de Cervantes."

Finally, by working in the prose poem form, and doing so with specifically local content, Azorín appropriates and in effect nationalizes this form, specifically in the mode developed by Baudelaire, reversing previous appropriations by French travelers of the book's subject matter. Martínez Cachero notes that part of Azorín's generation's desire to depict the Spanish landscape is:

> el propósito de dar cumplida réplica a tantos viajeros foráneos que a lo largo del siglo XIX nos habían visitado y, después, habían escrito sobre lo que habían visto; viajeros románticos y de años posteriores, de diferentes nacionalidades y, por desgracia, no tan atendible su testimonio como lo fuera el famoso *Viaje a España* de Teófilo Gautier, libro que (según Azorín) «ayudó a la juventud de 1898 a ver el paisaje de España» dado que «en lo que toca a la interpretación poética del paisaje, difícilmente será superado nunca, porque la geografía de la Península no está contada allí, sino vista, con visión absorta, desinteresada y esplendente». (Martínez Cachero 24)

Conversely, Azorín's application of this form to his subject matter is a gesture of aesthetic modernization of parts of Spain's geography, physical and cultural, that had remained peripheral to modernizing currents. This dimension of the book is reinforced by references to Spanish and French literature. Inman Fox has extensively studied the literary sources of Azorín's writings, even in his travel writings, and argues that "Azorín no halla la inspiración en la observación de la realidad, sino en otros libros" (*Ideología* 122). I would suggest that the literary allusions of *Los pueblos* (although fewer than in perhaps any other work) also have the function of establishing affinities and parity between Spanish and French literature, and implying that the appropriation he is enacting here, of the prose poem, is one between equals. Finally, Azorín also takes the modern prose poem out of its original urban context and applies its optic to provincial life. This translation gives his prose poetry a slightly parodic character, although the parodic quality is usually subordinated to genuine sentiment.

"La fiesta"

The opening article of *Los pueblos* is a memory of the future. A fictionalized version of the author, Don Joaquín, a poet, returns to his native village after a long absence. It is curious that *Los pueblos*, in contrast to *La ruta de Don Quijote*, begins with a return instead of a departure. The return home of Azorín himself (as the writer) is never recounted within the book, so structurally this fictionalized return fills that vacuum. Indirectly, Azorín is declaring a fundamental motive of his journey and writing: his desire to be recognized as a poet. While Jurkevich sees in Don Joaquín's blindness the importance that Azorín places on his painterly role as ekphrastic writer, if we look at Don Joaquín as a stand-in for the author, what we see in this character—as opposed to the writer who is setting out to discover and document the real Spain for the reader—is not the importance of seeing as much as the desire to be seen—that is, to be recognized and affirmed—and the anxiety of being forgotten.

The piece opens with Doña Juana's greeting and naming of the poet. The theme of recognition is further developed when

Doña Juana calls down her three daughters. Although the emphasis of the scene is on Don Joaquín's recognition and recollection of each girl from the past, the pathos of the scene lies in their inability to recognize him. While Don Joaquín is the first to recognize the naturalness of their having forgotten him, the contrast between his remembering and their forgetting is poignant. The anxious wish for recognition is made evident when Rafael, the supervisor of the family's crops, arrives. Don Joaquín asks him directly, "¿tú no te acordarás de mí? ¿No te acuerdas de Don Joaquín?" (12). Rafael, embarrassed, responds negatively. The piece concludes with Don Joaquín's unspoken thoughts on the fate of poets, which is to live, like cicadas, briefly in song, and to die forgotten in the winter of old age.

This almost parable-like vignette describes the author's desire to escape this fate, by means of acknowledging its likelihood in a text that will nonetheless survive him. The presence of the three daughters is a fairy-tale feature that adds to the rather dreamy mood of the piece, and recalls Antonio Azorín's friend Sarrió and his three daughters in *Antonio Azorín*, inviting identification between Azorín and Don Joaquín. This identification is developed in the following chapter.

"Sarrió"

The anxiety over being forgotten connects the first two pieces of *Los pueblos*. "Sarrió," like "La fiesta," begins with a return. The writer appears as a first-person character, and the lines between fictional and actual Azorín are blurred. He is on a visit to his friend Sarrió, a character from *Antonio Azorín*, who he finds has been suffering from a wasting illness and who only recognizes the writer with difficulty. Furthermore, he learns with great sadness that Sarrió's youngest daughter, Pepita, a special friend of Antonio Azorín in that novel, has since died. The death of Pepita and the illness of Sarrió, as well as the latter's difficulty in recognizing Azorín, continue the theme of the desire for recognition, and also possibly suggest Azorín's desire to distance himself from these earlier works. The writer is difficult to recognize perhaps not only because of Sarrió's illness, but because he has changed since writing *Antonio Azorín* and wishes to express this. He has changed from novelist to poet, and must learn to leave, in some sense, his previous production behind. He transforms the memory of these relationships, extensively recounted in *Antonio Azorín*, into a prose poem. That is, he brings them over into his new aesthetic, but does so only elegiacally. While the nominal subject is Sarrió, as Don Joaquín appears to be the subject of "La fiesta," the identity of the author himself is the underlying subject.

The piece opens and closes with descriptions of the small town and its plaza which is described as quiet but sensually vivid and light-filled, especially in comparison with Sarrió's shadowy house: "Yo he llegado a media mañana a este pueblo sosegado y claro; el sol ilumina la ancha plaza; unas sombras azules, frescas, caían en un ángulo de los aleros de las casas y bañaban las puertas" (14). The sky is "limpio, luminoso" (14). The reader pauses for a moment to enjoy the calm of the atmosphere, and the "ruido manso" of the fountain in the silence of the small-town morning. Sobejano's description of the second half of *Confesiones* as "presentánea" (2001, 498) seems an excellent one to describe the presentation of landscape throughout *Los pueblos*, and the evocation of the presence of place is intensified alternately by the fragility, delicateness, and fluidity of the subjects who briefly inhabit it, both the author himself and other characters.

The meeting between Azorín and his old friend is very sad. Sarrió is virtually unrecognizable due to the neglect of his appearance that illness has brought. This Sarrió, in contrast to the warm, lively epicure of *Antonio Azorín*, is a melancholy shadow. At the center of this scene, as in the previous vignette, is a character's inability to recognize the author:

> —¡Sarrió! ¡Sarrió!—le he gritado.
> Entonces él ha permanecido un momento absorto, mirándome con sus ojos apagados, blandos; después ha abierto la boca para decir algo que no acertaba a decir, y al fin ha exclamado con voz opaca, fría:
> —¡Ah, sí! Azorín... (21)

In this scene the failure of recognition of a close friend is more pathetic than the understandable inability of the girls to remember. As in other moments of the book, Azorín juxtaposes two treatments of the same theme, one lighter and one more profound. This melancholy interior scene is contrasted again with the landscape when Azorín reemerges into the tranquil afternoon, and the author explicitly shows how his reencounter with the identical landscape has been changed by the experience he has just had: "he vuelto a oír el susurro del agua, los gritos de las golondrinas que cruzan raudas por el cielo, las campanadas del viejo reloj que marca sus horas, rítmico, eterno, indiferente a los dolores del hombre..." (22). This contrast is at the center of the experience of landscape in *Los pueblos*. Juxtaposed with anecdotes of human suffering and fragility, the landscape is calm, self-contained, and indifferent, yet beautiful in just this, in its deep presence.

Again I wish to emphasize the importance of the theme of recognition in these opening vignettes. Throughout *Los pueblos*, the author plays a game of hide-and-seek with himself. He flirts with the anonymity of the provincial space, but again and again expresses fear of this anonymity and the desire for confirmation of his identity. This underlying game of hiding and revealing provides dramatic tension to these otherwise slight narratives. Finally, the almost exaggerated accumulation of deaths in this vignette is striking. Not only is Sarrió gravely ill, Pepita has also died. There was no indication of any failure of health in *Antonio Azorín*. Their deaths seem almost gratuitous, and unlikely in so short a space of elapsed time. It is clear that the author is not overly concerned with verisimilitude, and that his priority is to emphasize the fragility of life.

"La novia de Cervantes"

The tone of the following piece is much lighter and the mood softer, yet themes of identity and recognition and the delicacy of the self versus the sensual immediacy of the landscape persist. In this piece the changing landscape becomes a space for an almost fantastical fluidity of the traveler's identity. Having figuratively left his novelistic literary past behind in "Sarrió," Azorín begins "La novia" with a departure, by train, whose gaiety is described in detail. In this opening section Azorín fancies himself to be an anonymous bourgeois gentleman, an identity conferred on him by his fellow passengers. However, once he exits the train in the deserted Yeles station and finds himself faced with a long, solitary walk by moonlight to Esquivias, his fantasy evaporates: "Ya no soy el pequeño burgués que tiene un huerto con parrales y viaja con dos, con cuatro, con seis chicos rubios o morenos: ahora soy el pequeño filósofo que acepta resignado los designios ocultos e inexorables de las cosas" (27). But a different identity is conferred upon him again when he arrives at the inn and converses with the innkeeper: "Yo ya no soy un pequeño burgués [. . .] ni soy un pequeño filósofo [. . .]: ahora soy un pequeño comisionista de vinos" (28). His identity changes according to his circumstances and seems to have no stability.

These playful transformations prepare the way for the central metamorphosis of the account. The writer awakes the day after his journey to the sound of the church bells, which would be the same that Cervantes would have heard (30). Already Azorín is playing at blurring the distinction between similarity and identity. He falls back to sleep and is awakened by "las mismas campanas, el mismo acompañamiento clamoroso y la misma melopea" (30). The repetition of the word *misma* evokes the notion of identity. The fancifulness of this idea is followed by an intimation of mystery exuded by a neighboring house: "uno de estos típicos caserones manchegos, cerrados siempre, que muestra sus tres balcones viejos, con las maderas despintadas, misteriosas, inquietadoras" (30). This description echoes both Sarrió's house, one of those closed, dark houses the author finds so common in the Castilian provinces, and the mysterious house he is about to encounter, which is full of transporting light and order.

The author's arrival at this house echoes his arrivals in the previous two articles, but at those houses he was acquainted with the inhabitants. Here he knows no one, but he is nonetheless received with strange naturalness: "ahora me parece lógico, naturalísimo, el que esta dama me haya invitado a trasponer los umbrales. Todo, desde la nebulosa, estaba dispuesto para que una dama silenciosa invitara a entrar en su casa a un filósofo no menos silencioso" (35). Finally, the author will have the uncanny impression of being in the presence of Cervantes's betrothed, in the person of the present daughter of the household. However, he is careful to assert at the article's end that this young woman is a distinct individual, naming both women and reflecting that it was his imagination that led him to the imaginative confusion. Similarly, the physical elements of the environment—architecture, geography—facilitate an experience of fluidity, of mysterious connectedness, of identity between distinct times and distinct individuals, but Azorín's framing of the piece in the space of a day, from sunrise to sunset, establishes the specific historic moment of the experience. Through an act of imagination, landscape becomes a kind of structure that allows a temporary imaginative escape from the bonds of time and individual identity.

"Los toros"

This article, dedicated to the painter Zuloaga, has a *costumbrista* flavor, but Azorín takes the customs vignette and deepens it, marginalizing the traditional content (here, the bullfights) and introducing, if humoristically, the existential theme of identity, which connects it to the previous pieces. Here, the author pays a visit to his friend Don Tomás and his family who are preparing for an outing to a bullfight. The encounter opens, once again, with the naming of the protagonist by a character in the vignette, establishing his presence there. Don Tomás is going through a stack of hatboxes at the top of his closet, reviewing as he does so the moments in history that he associates with each hat. He explains that he has purchased so many hats over the years because between his infrequent trips to the cities his hats go out of style. His hats thus identify him as having belonged at moments to the city but also as being fundamentally an outsider there. Furthermore, these aide memoires are losing their effectiveness; he is glad to have a friend to help him remember, although Azorín's memory seems equally vague.

The women of the house are equally subject to changing fashions. They are anxiously conferring about how they should wear their flowers, and refer to the advice of a fashion columnist. The gravity of the issue for both men and women is a bit comical. Their lives depend on fashions created far from their homes, transmitted through the press. Their anxious attentiveness to fashion, like Don Tomás's to his hats, gives them a sense of connection to the urban world but also reveals their distance from it.

This is the first time the theme of the press appears in *Los pueblos*. Azorín downplays his identity as a writer in his self-descriptions, but he points to the fact with these references to the press. Here the readers of the press are female, and it would seem Azorín has a fondness for female readers. One may think of Pepita, Sarrió's daughter, who was a reader of magazines and later his letters from the capital, an analogous relationship to the urban columnist and his readership in the provinces. His affection for female characters as well as for aging and otherwise isolated characters in *Los pueblos* indicates both his personal affinities with these politically marginal segments of society and also helps establish his characterization of the provinces, which are defined precisely by their marginality to the metropolis.

Many of the essays in *Los pueblos* seem organized in thematic pairs, the first of each pair being a somewhat light introduction to the theme of the second. The first two of the book are linked by Sarrió and the theme of death; the second, although less obviously, by the poignancy of the woman as intimate reader-listener. At the conclusion of "La novia de Cervantes," Azorín reflects on the unknown words that Cervantes would have spoken to his wife on twilight walks on the plains of La Mancha, and alleges that these "palabras simples, palabras vulgares" were "más grandes que todos las palabras de sus libros" (39). Writing this here as a journalist, within a piece intended for journalistic publication, Azorín reveals the value that he nonetheless places on intimate language, and his desire to achieve some of the same intimacy with readers in this context of mass communication. He affects a form of masquerade—public writing as private writing—to attempt to reduce the impersonality of the relationship between public writer and reader.

The theme of precarious individuality in "Los toros" is evoked visually at the article's end when the storm that has been threatening all day breaks: "Y comienza una lluvia densa, cerrada. Allá abajo, en la feria, la gente corre despavorida y abre precipitadamente los paraguas" (46). In the visual depiction of the crowd each person loses his individuality—that individuality so carefully cultivated by Don Tomás with his hats and Juanita with her corsage—and each is now defined by the same object, his umbrella.

"El buen juez"

In "El buen juez" Azorín does not appear directly, although he is implicitly present in the quote of Marquina that serves as the piece's epigraph: "Azorín, ¿quiere usted decir algo de las sentencias del presidente Magnaud?"[18] The question rather echoes those of the Conde Lucanor, and indeed what follows is a kind of exemplary tale. Inspired by Magnaud's book, the "good judge" will change his mind about a case he is deliberating, causing a small scandal in his provincial city.

Although the author disappears in this piece, themes of identity, recognition and validation are nonetheless present. This time, rather humorously, the narrative of recognition belongs to the little book that makes its way from the publisher in Barcelona (in translation from French) to a dusty bookshop window in Ciudad Real, to the judge's personal library where it is at odds with the various law tomes but cordially welcomed by *Don Quijote*. The book's journey of chance, from the city to the province, where it will ultimately make an important difference in the secret history of humanity, parallels the author's journey

---

[18] Paul Magnaud (1848–1926), "the good judge," president of the tribunal of Chateau, known for his personal and free sentences and his belief that the law should be interpretedly humanly. His *Sentences* were published in 1903.

from capital to province, where he hopes to have an impact as a writer.

"El buen juez," like "Los toros," has a *costumbrista* feel. The description of local manners and interiors outweighs the landscape here, and the author's humorous description of the women of the judge's family, with their exaggerated consternation before his intellectual revolution, recalls Larra's satiric writings. The general public, as well, is scandalized before the arrival of "una partícula de justicia" (61). As in "Los toros," Azorín uses the *cuadro de costumbres* while introducing greater depth into this genre. Here the judge's smile is symbolic of a noble attitude to the mysteries of human society, and the author suggests that this smile is of the first magnitude of importance in the secret history of humanity: "esa sonrisa extraordinaria, inmensa, que sólo le es dable contemplar a la Humanidad cada dos o tres siglos…" (61). Azorín's creative use of the *cuadro de costumbres* as the basis for a number of his poems is perhaps one of the most original elements in his personal elaboration of the prose poem.

There are few landscape passages in the piece, but Azorín evokes the feeling of a small provincial city: the casino, well ordered home and solicitous family, the "pintorescos gritos" (53) of the carbon vendor and the baker, "la suculenta torrija" (54) that hovers on the fork in the air as Don Alonso muses over the act he is about to carry out. In sum, the physical landscape seems less important than the social landscape in this piece. This social landscape is solid and comfortable, but it also resists the impression of something new.

The conclusion of "El buen juez" is slightly ambiguous. Was the judge's novel ruling the supreme and also final act of his life, given that the author notes that "ha sonreído, por última vez" (61)? This ambiguity is another possible example of the exaggerated number of deaths in *Los pueblos*. In conclusion, the author seems to decidedly prefer an elegiac perspective for describing his subjects, and the next chapter is perhaps the best example of this.

"Una elegía"

The poetry of *Los pueblos* rests in the contrast between individual lives, ephemeral and fluid, and the sensuous specificity of landscape. While the landscape may seem to resonate with the emotion of the observer, it is ultimately indifferent. But its distance, its wholeness and profundity beyond human histories, also brings solace. "Una elegía" is in part about the landscape's resistance to human impression, and human beings' persistence, in spite of this, to remember and be remembered. The photograph is a metaphor for both the fragility and the persistence of the individual.

The piece opens once again with the addressing of the narrator, this time by the reader, inserted momentarily as a character and a presence in the text. This reiterates the importance of the affirmation of the writer by the reader. After this brief evocation, however, the narrator cedes to the description of Julín. The evocation of Julín by her name contrasts with the insistence upon the narrator's name in the previous pieces, and at the same time, the diminutive name links the two. Julín is one of the many romantic young girls Azorín likes to recall in *Los pueblos*. Despite her misleadingly ambiguous name, Julín "era una muchacha delgada, esbelta, con unos grandes ojos melancólicos, azules..." (62). This delicate image is followed by a panegyric to the blacksmith's art. The durability of the iron being forged contrasts with the fragility of the girl who died tragically young. This juxtaposition is repeated throughout the piece. It concludes with a subject that combines the concepts of durability and fragility: the art of photography. Azorín recalls how when he arrives in a new town, he frequently visits the local photography shop. In this case he visits his photographer friend Don Baltasar, and sees a photo of Julín in his shop. Julín's pose and setting are described with detail. The piece concludes with the author listening to the church bells and meditating on the sadness of the passing of beauty. The church bells, like the photographer's art, synthesize ideas of durability; the strength and solidity of the metal outlive the vibrant peals that die away in the landscape, and that mark the passage of time. This contrast, and its momentary synthesis, is at the heart of the book's poetic structure.

The theme of resistance in the landscape to individual memory is taken up again in "En Loyola," where evidence of the saint's existence has been virtually erased by the heavy-handed interpretations of the monastery's modern curators. The observer must perform an act of imaginative archeology to rescue the authentic self from its current deformation.

"Un trasnochador"

"Un trasnochador" is a humoristic version of "El buen juez" and "El grande hombre del pueblo," and is placed symmetrically between them, separated by one article on each side. The subject of "Un trasnochador," as in the other two pieces, is a small-town gentleman whose environment is limiting for his personality. However, whereas the town's more "heroic" subjects find ways to productively invest their energy and talent, Don Juan lacks productive focus for his energy. He spends his nights in a tightly constricted circle of activities that lead endlessly back to the casino. When the tedium of this routine has exhausted him, he concludes the evening with a small tertulia in his kitchen over a late-night meal. The novelty of this piece is in the moonlit landscape of the town streets, whose mysterious ambience seems to anticipate a more significant event that never occurs: "La luz de la luna, suave, plateada, baña las fachadas de las casas; de los aleros, de los balcones, caen unas sombras largas, puntiagudas, sobre los blancos muros. Las lechuzas, en la torre de la iglesia, lanzan a intervalos misteriosos resoplidos" (69-70). The landscape here is similar to the plain with its suggestively mysterious house that the young Martínez Ruiz observed as a schoolboy through the window of his incarceration. Both landscapes are the repository of indefinite fantasies and longings for something that is lacking in the immediate social environment.

The above summaries show that the will to self-creation and affirmation in the environment is as strong in *Los pueblos* as in the Antonio Azorín trilogy. Even when the individual existence in question is not that of the author, enough parallels are established between author and other to sense a projected personal desire.

One last theme I would like to comment is the application of the prose poem format with its urban optic to the space of provincial Spain, and the affirmation of this form within the context of peninsular literature. The use of conventions of the prose poem to describe a provincial environment results in a slightly parodic tone. The best example of this is perhaps "El pez y el reloj." Here, the author most obviously imitates the Baudelairian flaneur, but the subject of his observation is the imitative elegance of the provinces. The departure from Azorín's normal perspective for his impersonation of the flaneur is evident in his uncommon interest in the elegant ladies. The various nuisances he encounters—especially of having to pay someone each time he sits in a beach chair—accentuate the gap between true luxury and the purchased second-rate elegance of the seaside resort. The influence of Baudelaire is unmistakable here, yet the piece is, curiously, dedicated to Luis Gabaldón.[19]

---

[19] Probably the Spanish playwright Luis Gabaldón y Blanco (1869–?).

The evocation of Spanish writers—Gabaldón, Cervantes, the author of the Lazarillo, Pereda almost surely in "La velada"—in equal part with French writers—Montaigne, Baudelaire, Magnaud—reflects Azorín's gesture of nationalizing the prose poem form. Form (French) is imposed on Spanish provincial space and the result is an original synthesis, not mere imitation, and this is reinforced by the parity in references to French and Spanish letters.

La ruta de Don Quijote

Like *Los pueblos*, *La ruta de Don Quijote* is a collection of articles based on travel experiences, and features the self-presentation of the writer, although it neither continues the strikingly original poetic mode that Azorín initiated in the Antonio Azorín saga and brought to maturity in *Los pueblos* (with a few exceptions), nor does it show equal innovation in descriptive technique. While Valverde deems *Los pueblos* a "libro impar, el mejor, sin duda, firmado con el nombre Azorín, y quizá el mejor absoluto del autor" (264), with respect to the articles commissioned by *El Imparcial* in March 1905 he says "las crónicas más ceñidas al tema del viaje se quedan en cierta ambigüedad: ni tienen el valor de estampa como *Los pueblos*, ni son comentario al *Quijote* —más adelante, en innumerables artículos, Azorín llegará a ser el mejor crítico literario de la obra cervantina" (267). The determinist ideas in *La ruta* have been critiqued by Herbert Ramsden. Martínez Cachero observes that "*La ruta*: contradice una de las cuatro condiciones señaladas por el escritor metido a viajero, el cual debe dejar que pase el tiempo y así podrá escribir con la lejanía temporal y espacial necesarias para que su testimonio resulte más limpio o (con otras palabras) despojado de peligrosa inmediatez" (28). Perhaps as a consequence of the time restrictions Azorín faced while writing these articles, there is not the same degree of formal or technical innovation as in *Los pueblos* in these pieces.

One difference between the descriptive passages in *La ruta* and those in the previous books lies in their increased dynamism with respect to movement in both time and space. Azorín had already realized some marvelous moving landscapes, such as his departure by train to Toledo and his walk through Las Ventas in *La voluntad*. Moving perspective is much more important in *La ruta*, as it is explicitly a series of travelogues, and he must convey a sense of movement through space and the elapse of time. This he does very effectively. In "En marcha," his trip from Madrid to Argamasilla by train is an account of the plain observed from the passenger's window. The experience of space becomes almost rhythmic as certain details emerge and disappear at intervals: "De cuando en cuando, se divisan la paredes blancas, refulgentes, de una casa; se ve perderse a lo lejos, rectos, inacabables, los caminos. Y una cruz tosca de piedra nos recuerda, en esta llanura solitaria, monótona, yerma, desesperante, el sitio de una muerte, de una tragedia" (84). The polyvalence of the words such as "desesperante" and "monótona" are especially effective, since they can refer not only to the landscape but also to the experience of the traveler. The roads that lead to unknown parts, the hermetic houses, and the cross imbue the landscape with a suggestive atmosphere of mystery. Traveling is a departure into the unknown, and Azorín captures this act of setting out very effectively.

In other passages, his descriptions accurately reflect his mode of transport. In "Primera salida," Azorín travels "en un diminuto y destartalado carro," pulled by "una jaca microscópica" (111). The landscape is similar to that observed from the train: "la llanura ancha, la llanura infinita, la llanura desesperante, se ha extendido ante nuestra vista [. . .] acá y allá, refulgiendo al sol, destacaban las paredes blancas, nítidas, de las casas diseminadas en la campiña" (112). Here, the temporal adverb, "de cuando en cuando," is replaced by the spatial reference, "acá y allá" (112). What predominates in this account of an almost maddeningly slow journey is space over time, and indeed, time seems difficult to mark in a space with such sparse visual elements by which to gauge time's passage. The plain lacks even trees that might otherwise be periodic markers. Martínez Cachero has observed that Cervantes's text: "sirve, a más de referente inexcusable, de materia propicia para llenar el vacío o animar la monotonía que parecen producirse en una marcha donde el viajero, a su paso, no encuentra personas con las que conversar ni objetos que describir" (40). "Primera salida" is a good example of this. We see from some of the repeated details that Azorín is in danger of evoking only the same monotonous landscape, and although he has a companion, the conversation the latter offers is very scant, limited to answering Azorín's questions about agricultural practices. We find here, therefore, an interior meditation on the possible effect of these plains upon Alonso Quijano. Space is equated directly with state of mind: "¿De qué manera no sentir que un algo misterioso, que un anhelo que no podemos explicar, que un ansia indefinida, inefable, surge en nuestro espíritu? Esta ansiedad, este anhelo, es la llanura" (114). Interior and exterior are conflated.

Authorial self-representation is one of the features that link *La ruta* to *Los pueblos* and also to the Antonio Azorín saga. In the first article, "La partida," Azorín describes his conversation about his imminent departure with his landlady, Doña Isabel. His departure is not characterized by anticipation, as might be expected, but by a melancholy feeling. He explains that "no tengo más remedio que marcharme a los pueblos" (78). His mood seems related to the pressures of his writer's profession. "Yo creo, Azorín," declares Doña Isabel, "que esos libros y esos papeles le están a usted matando. Muchas veces—añade sonriendo—he tenido la tentación de quemarlos todos durante alguno de sus viajes" (78). Thus, of course, Azorín sets up a parallel between himself and the great writer who has inspired this journey, but his anxiety about being a writer, and the conflict between public and private identity, has already been a recurrent theme in his writings. As Valverde puts it:

> El periodismo ha llevado a J. Martínez Ruiz a ser escritor creativo, pero también le estorba para serlo. Llegará a una transacción: a ser «colaborador literario» de periódicos, más bien que periodista propiamente dicho, pero toda su obra quedará sujeta a los límites formales y materiales de la Prensa, incluso cuando se escribe para ser publicada directamente en libro. (228)

The voice in this book is very similar to that of *Las confesiones*. The "little philosopher" could be said to be the protagonist of this book, although in the protestation of modesty that concludes the first article one can almost here the voice of Antonio Azorín in his letters to Pepita: "Lector: perdóname; yo soy un pobre hombre que, en los ratos de vanidad, quiere aparentar que sabe algo, pero que en realidad no sabe nada" (81). Azorín seems eager to establish a sympathetic relationship with the reader. Furthermore, he apparently wishes to collapse any implicit hierarchical relationship between reader and writer.

The persona of the writer here is not as complex as in *Los pueblos*. After the initial self-description, he appears in two ways. His verbal presence consists mainly of brief exchanges with the people he encounters along the way, to whom he usually addresses questions, and in frequent questions directed to the reader. His physical presence is established in several ways: through allusions to his physical state, often to discomfort or weariness, through his descriptions of himself struggling to write in rustic conditions, and through others' reactions to him. This is seen in the portrait of Martín, who responds somewhat mischievously to the introduction of Azorín as a journalist who can put him in the papers, "¿Conque este señor puede hacer que Martín, sin salir de su casa, vaya muy largo?" (110). This is, in effect, what Azorín the writer of these pages is doing for the readers of *El Imparcial*. He also causes commotion as a writer in "Los Sanchos de Criptana," where this peculiar fraternity hopes that Azorín might use his influence to publish their hymn for the Cervantine Centennial: "¿cree usted que este himno puede tener algún éxito?," Don Bernardo asks. In both cases, Azorín's identity as writer is both what has brought him into contact with his company, but also what establishes a barrier between them.

Only in one part does a moment of genuinely sympathetic connection seem to occur, with Don José Antonio in "La venta de Puerto Lápiche" (115). Valverde opines that "[l]o mejor del libro, probablemente, son los tipos, tengan o no conexión con el tema quijotesco—Ambiente en Argamasilla, Siluetas de Argamasilla—, dignos siempre de figurar en *Los Pueblos*" (267). To this list I would add "La venta de Puerto Lápiche." This article shares some of the characteristics of *Los pueblos*: elegiac quality, parallels between author and third-person subject, and landscape as vibrant presence in contrast to the tenuousness of human life.

In "La Venta de Puerto Lápiche," Azorín seeks out the doctor and long-time resident Don José Antonio. Azorín describes Don José Antonio with greater detail than any other person whom he meets in his travels. But even more significant is the doctor's smile: "una de esas sonrisas inconfundibles, llenas de bondad, llenas de luz, llenas de una vida interna intensa, tal vez de resignación, tal vez de hondo dolor" (116). This smile relates him to other personalities Azorín has treated with affection, such as Pascual Verdú and the Good Judge. Azorín has come to consult with the doctor about the possible location of the inn that no longer exists. Don José Antonio, besides being the town doctor, has also been the sole writer and editor of a town newspaper, in which he has written on the subject of the inn. The newspaper is on such a modest scale that he writes it out himself by hand, and brings it to the casino on Sundays. After the other members have perused it, he carries it home and files it away "para que la colección no quede descabalada" (118). Later the writers walk to where the inn might have stood. The space is now "un gran relleno donde crecen las plantas silvestres" (118). Azorín inwardly speculates on how the inn might have been in Cervantes' time, overflowing with activity. Yet it is not only the contrast between the memory of the famous inn and the abandoned spot that marks where it might have stood that produces the melancholic tone in the piece. The good doctor, Don José Antonio, is also disappearing, it seems. His cough is a symptom of an illness and Don José Antonio "sabe que no se ha de curar; los dolores atroces han ido poco a poco purificando su carácter; toda su vida está hoy en sus ojos y en su sonrisa" (120). This modest man, whose intellectual work has almost no resonance in the world and yet who patiently continues, faces death with stoic resignation. The piece concludes with a melancholy evocation of the landscape, as Azorín departs from the town: "Y yo he columbrado a lo lejos, en la blancura de la carretera, cómo desaparecía este buen amigo de una hora, a quien no veré más [. . .]" (120).

This piece is certainly worthy of *Los pueblos*, and coincides with them in the ways mentioned. But there is another difference between this and the other pieces in *La ruta* that may be revealing. Unlike most of the types Azorín describes here, Don José Antonio belongs to the educated, provincial, middle class. There is a tone of formality, and a sense of genuine respect in his interaction with Don José Antonio that is not always present in his other interactions, which are characterized by a casual joviality that at the same time does not lead to true camaraderie, or by a formality that seems somewhat ironic, as with the Sanchos of Criptana.

Unamuno's *paisajes sueltos*: a new mode of writing

Studies of landscape in Unamuno's writings have tended to study the subject across the various genres Unamuno practiced (such as Blanco Aguinaga's essential study *El Unamuno contemplativo*). With respect to the few specific studies of Unamuno's collections of landscape articles, Manuel Alvar's introduction to his 1966 edition of *Paisajes*, Llorén's García's study of Unamuno's travel writings, and Richard Cardwell's study of *Andanzas* are very valuable. However, the study of these works as a body also requires a consideration of the different modes of writing that these pieces (some of which cannot even be called in rigor travel writings) embody. Unamuno's landscape articles can be roughly divided into two groups. First, there are those articles in which the essayistic, discursive element is dominant. This group includes many of the articles in *Por tierras de Portugal y de España*—and almost all of those dedicated to Portugal—as well as a number of the articles in *Andanzas*. The second group consists of articles in which the emphasis seems to be on the communication of intimate, vital experiences to the reader. These writings, especially those in the latter part of *Andanzas* resemble a combination of spiritual diary and manual.

Paisajes

Paisajes was published in 1902, but the individual pieces date back to 1897 (Lloréns García 32). Its unity consists in the proximity of the places described to Salamanca, Unamuno's recently adopted new home (Lloréns García 33). I have already discussed some of the articles in *Paisajes* in chapter 1, including "El sentimiento de la naturaleza," which functions as a prologue to the collection. To summarize briefly, some of the principal points of this essay are 1) the antiquity of the experience of nature, despite the only recent full consciousness and aesthetic representation of this experience; 2) the necessity of emancipation from total dependence upon the land and the possession of some leisure for the conscious experience and appreciation of nature to be possible; 3) the struggle between city and country as embodiments of the agricultural versus the pastoral way of life respectively, the pastoral life being associated with Christ. The essay is divided into three parts, and the middle section is devoted to La Flecha, a favorite spot of Fray Luis de León, to whom Unamuno attributes the emergence of the expression of nature in Spanish literature: "Este sentimiento castellano de la naturaleza llega en Fray Luis de León a cobrar conciencia de sí y a revelarse expresándose en forma limpidísima y transparente" (OC I, 30).

La Flecha was not only Fray Luis's site of refuge from the conflicts of society, but a place of cordial companionship. In a situation that reflects Unamuno's life, Los nombres de Cristo opens in June, after the close of an academic year. The friends retire to an orchard: "Pues entrados en ella, primero y por un espacio pequeño se anduvieron paseando y gozando al frescor, y después se sentaron junto a la sombra de unas parras y junto a la corriente de una pequeña fuente en ciertos asientos" (32). The landscape as a site of cordial companionship is important in Unamuno's writings. Some of Unamuno's most felt landscape writings imply a desire for a different model of relationship with the reader, one characterized by sympathy, understanding and warmth. Like Azorín, Unamuno, in his travel writings, ponders openly the conflicts between his public and private self. In his travel writings he speaks from his private, intimate self, which he establishes through self-description and tone.

"Brianzuelo de la Sierra," the second piece of the book, is the first travel article properly speaking, as it recounts a specific trip. In this playful article, Unamuno does not wish to be roused from bed by his friend to explore the town at which they arrived the previous night: "¡A soñarlo! Déjame que me le figure a mi antojo" (41). However, when Unamuno's companion protests that "Lo mismo podías habértele figurado en la ciudad" (41), Unamuno objects that "No; lo mismo no. Aquí estoy en él y la conciencia de estar en él vivifica mi imaginación" (41). In this passage we see two key features of Unamuno's ideas about landscape. First, there is a blurry distinction between internal and external landscapes, and second, the perception of landscape is not a passive but rather a creative act. However, it is clear that for Unamuno, appreciation of landscape requires physical contact. Vital experience thus becomes a requisite part of the process of landscape writing, a residue that the writing somehow contains. Since experience can also be feigned, of course, in literature, there is a bond of trust between travel writer and reader. The reader expects that the writer is sharing real experiences with him or her, and part of travel writings' value consists in this condition. The value of travel writing, like open-air landscape painting, depends, unlike most other literary forms, on this extra-textual condition.

The theme of blurred boundaries between interior and exterior landscapes is continued in Unamuno and his companions' encounter with the village woman who appears to be contemplating the valley from the front door of her house. Unamuno muses aloud: "¿Cómo se irá posando el valle en el espíritu de esa pobre vieja?" (43). His companion dismisses his ponderings, arguing that she must know the view by heart. Unamuno converts the conventional figure of speech of "by heart" (de memoria) into a metaphor:"Sí, el valle será un pedazo de su alma, el escenario de ella, acaso; si se lo quitaran moriría… de seguro" (43). The vision is so vitally important that she would perish without it. The friend's comment that she must "know it by heart" is proven true when they learn that she is blind. Ironically, she herself says that she spends her time "viendo el valle" (43), although when asked to clarify says that it is "como si lo viera" (43). Interior and exterior, reality and imagination, subject and object—the conventional distinctions are deliberately blurred.

In "Puesta de Sol," Unamuno recalls a magnificent sunset he witnessed returning to Salamanca on a walk. The feeling this sunset invoked is an example both of the blurring of boundaries between interior and exterior and of the substantiality Unamuno gives to interior experience: "La calma que en invisible lluvia caía de los cielos y en insensible vapor subía de la tierra, era el ambiente íntimo del momento" (47). This description echoes Unamuno's earlier description of the experience of rain, as a phenomenon that must evoke a primitive memory of relief: "El deleitoso esponjamiento espiritual con que nos regala el ver caer lentamente, cual si se derritiera el cielo sobre la tierra, el extenso manto de la lluvia, a cuyo recibimiento parece dilatarse la llanura, dando luego, como en expansión de gozo y en hacimiento de gracias, más penetrantes sus aromas" (29). But calm is only an interior experience, to which Unamuno gives metaphorical substantiality in the landscape. The metaphor of absorption, the relation between rain and fertility, conveys the experience of the landscape as nourishing, both in a maternal way and in a divine, paternal way (mana).

Another feature of this piece is Unamuno's confession of his inadequacy to represent the scene he witnessed. He declares his wish to be able to paint the scene so that he would not have to settle with "el restrajo" (49) the experience has left behind. This is more than an artist's modesty. A key feature of these intimate writings is that they point to experience outside the writing. It is the experience itself that he is interested in conveying, an experience to which the texts points but cannot substitute. The text supports the communication of experience. It is a tool, not an end. Furthermore, Unamuno emphasizes not the particularity of his experience, but rather its universality. The contemplation of the sunset makes him feel united with the history of humanity:

> Aquel rayo de la gloria de las edades siderales, arrebatándome a las congojas de mi carrera cotidiana y al mezquino compás de la realidad de cada día, resucitó bajo los abismos de la conciencia y sobre la roca viva de su sedimiento, los remotos espíritus de los abuelos de mis abuelos, la cándida niñez del linaje humano. (48)

Unamuno emphasizes what is universal in his experience of the landscape. He invites identity, not just empathy, from his reader. He is not writing now as artist or intellectual but as human being, to a reader who has equal access, at least potentially, to this type of experience. Thus his landscape writings are not mere accounts of a particular experience, but a kind of exemplary writing, in which he models a type of experience for the reader.

Unamuno's vision of the landscape is rooted in a Christian perspective. As Alvar writes, Unamuno discovered the Castilian landscape "desde el cristianismo" (Lloréns 31). In "Fantasía crepuscular" the local landscape that surrounds him makes Unamuno recall the world as divine text as described in Genesis (53). Manuel Alvar observes that Unamuno "[n]o sólo ha buscado la fusión del hombre con su tierra, sino que, incluso, ha llegado a identificar la patria con Dios, con lo que la hipóstasis final se reducía—y simplificaba—las diferencias que pudieron presentarse al formular como metáfora lo que es identificación" (13). Returning to "Visión crespuscular," Unamuno describes the activity of contemplation of the landscape as "aquel oficio tan doméstico cuanto religioso" (53). The religious dimension differentiates these texts from other literary forms that they also resemble (prose poem, essay, travel diary etc.).

Por tierras de Portugal y de España: Portugal

First published as a collection in 1911, *Por tierras de Portugal y de España* is markedly different from *Paisajes*. The section dedicated to Portugal seems more closely related to *En torno al casticismo*; that is, it is more an essayistic interpretation of Portuguese culture, with a largely determinist perspective. The section on Spain is somewhat more place-based. However, the articles throughout are in general more essayistic than poetic in tone and character. They are also heavily infused with literary references. The articles in *Por tierras de Portugal y de España* at times resemble literary criticism, in the manner of Azorín's *El paisaje de España visto por los españoles.*

The opening article, "Eugenio de Castro," contains the nucleus of his vision of Portugal, at which he arrives through a reading of various literary texts. The practice of reading, especially the classics, as a means of studying national character, was common to the Generation of 1898.

> As Ramsden explains: in their reading of literature as in their travels their emphasis is on 'lo eterno de la casta,' 'lo típico y lo característico', 'la continuidad nacional'. 'De cada país,' writes Unamuno, 'me interesan los [escritores] que más del país son, los más castizos, los más propios (1910; III, 544). The great writer, like the exceptional historian, holds up, as it were, a mirror to collective consciousness. (Ramsden, *The 1898 Movement* 157)

For Unamuno, one of the most representative texts of the Portuguese spirit is de Castro's *Constança*, published in 1900: "Parece como si su mano al escribirla se hubiese convertido en el arpa eólica del pueblo, vibrando al soplo del alma de éste. La lírica de *Constança* es la más alta y la más noble lírica, aquella que, siendo profundamente colectiva, es, por eso mismo, profundamente personal" (297). The end of this quote reflects

Unamuno's belief in an identification of the artist as individual with his society.

What Unamuno finds most poignant, and most Portuguese, about de Castro's poem, is the figure of Constança herself. In most accounts of Don Pedro's tumultuous love life, and especially Camoens', attention has been focused upon the prince's adulterous passion, "como mucho más interesante y más poética que la otra," being "más de espectáculo, más visible y más aparatosa" (298). However, the story of the faithful, rejected spouse is equally as tragic, he argues, although "es una tragedia íntima y silenciosa" (298). It is easy to recognize in Unamuno's sentimental preference for Constança his vision of the intrahistoric. Constança, in her narrative of (historical) marginality, and her humble faithfulness, shares affinities with the intrahistoric pueblo that Unamuno described in *En torno al casticismo*. Over the epic (Camoens), Unamuno argues for the lyric as the most representative of the Portuguese spirit, and this lyrical essence is intimately linked to what he sees as Portugal's melancholy spirit expressed in word "saudade." Unamuno sees Portugal as an intrinsically melancholy country: "El culto al dolor parece ser uno de los sentimientos más característicos de este melancólico y saudoso Portugal" (299). With respect to landscape, Unamuno does note that in Constança "aparece por dondequiera, templando y serenando el cuadro, el paisaje estupendo de Coimbra, de esa maravilla de Coimbra, de la que guardo un imperecedero recuerdo [. . .], recorriendo en compañía de Castro las riberas del Mondego" (301).

In his essay on Teixeira de Pascoaes he invokes "días arrancados al tiempo" (311) spent with the poet in his family home, including the beautiful view of the Támega River that the poet drinks in from his window each day. He does describe O Bon Jesús do Monte and Guarda in detail, but these descriptions are more satirical than lyrical. Of the latter, which he describes as "[u]na cosa para encantar a los honrados comerciantes portugueses que van allá a pasar el domingo, a los brasileños y hasta a los ingleses" (365), he laments: "¡Qué difícil de educar es el sentimiento de la naturaleza! [. . .] lo bonito es enemigo de lo hermoso" (366). With respect to Guarda, a border town off the tourist route whose walls glimpsed through a train window had peaked his curiosity on other trips, Unamuno is even harsher: "[E]n resumidas cuentas, el fruto mayor que de mi visita a Guarda he sacado es el poder decir alguna vez, cuando de Guarda se hable o se la miente: también la he visto" (380).

"Las ánimas del Purgatorio en Portugal," and even more so "Un pueblo suicida," are heart-wrenching essays. One of the novelties of Unamuno's writings on Portugal is in fact this essayistic entry into dark emotional territory, and it is possible that this exploration of emotional register is reflected in *Del sentimiento trágico de lavida*. Another difference from *En torno al casticismo* is Unamuno's choice of primarily nineteenth- and twentieth-century texts as representative of the Portuguese spirit, in contrast to his selection of Golden Age texts as most characteristic of Spain.

In "La pesca de Espinho," Unamuno describes an unexpected scene in a fishing area of Aveiro. On the beach pairs of oxen pull the fishing boats onto the shore:

> Esto de sacar las redes con parejas de bueyes es lo que más carácter da a la pesca de Espinho, asemejándola a una labor agrícola y prestando asidero a la imaginación para cotejar con la labor de los campos en esta región en que, como digo, el mar parece se ruraliza. (347)

Unamuno analyzes the surprising conjunction of sea and agriculture in the scene, the different yoking practices in Portugal and in Spain, the significance of the yokes themselves, ornate and traditional, which will soon be museum items, fishing practices, and the curious fate of crabs and other sea life carried away by the estuaries to later be found in piles inland, fertilizing the earth as they decompose. All of these elements are brought together towards the end as Unamuno witnesses a splendid sunset, and their final meaning is summed up when Unamuno considers the past maritime glories of Portugal:

> ¡Qué tristeza infunde, después de recorrer con la memoria la espléndida historia de las glorias marinas de Portugal, la patria de los más grandes navegantes, fijar la vista en estos pobres mansos bueyecitos rubios tirando playa arriba las cuerdas de las redes, sumisos sus astados testuces bajo los ornamentos yugos, en cuyo centro brilla el blasón, un tiempo resplandeciente de gloria, de Portugal! (353).

This is one of Unamuno's essays in the section on Portugal that most approaches a poetic quality.

Finally, in "Guarda" especially, we do see Unamuno present himself as a writer, here to complain of the impositions of his profession: "Es cosa terrible esto de ver algo para escribir de ello, más bien que escribir porque se ha visto. Pero el oficio…" (374-375). He also describes his dinner companions' curiosity about him as he writes his notes in a notebook: "¿Y no es acaso uno de los encantos en los viajes el de intrigar a los que nos ven y, si es posible, hacerse pasar por personaje misterioso?" (379). These self-descriptions recall those of Azorín in *La ruta de Don Quijote*. Unamuno, by presenting himself this way, invites the reader to step to experience the journey not just as recipient of an account, but also as a privileged companion.

Por tierras de Portugal y de España: Spain

The essays devoted to Spain in *Por tierras de Portugal y de España* are, like those dedicated to Portugal, characteristically more discursive and less descriptive than those in *Paisajes*. In format, they are more characteristically travel writings than the essays on Portugal (of which only "Braga," "O Bon Jesús Do Monte," "Guarda," and "Alcobaça" are more conventional travel writings, that is, with a clear sense of movement, of arrivals, encounters, and departures). It is in *Por tierras de Portugal y de España* that Unamuno makes his famous statement on the purpose of travel: "Estas excursiones no son sólo un consuelo, un descanso y una enseñanza; son además, y acaso sobre todo, uno de los mejores medios de cobrar amor y apego a la patria" (433).

The general difference between the more discursive articles in the Spanish section of *Por tierras de Portugal y de España* and those of *Andanzas* is in part explained by the distinction Lloréns García makes between two dimensions of Unamuno's "obra paisajístico-viajera" (34): that between his writings as a "viajero urbano" and a "viajero-peregrino." As Lloréns García has studied, Unamuno had a well articulated theory of travel, which he carried out in practice. Lloréns summarizes the main dimensions of Unamuno's travel writings:

> Unamuno es consciente de la labor que realiza viajando: es excursionista-montañero para descubrir enteramente la patria y obtener de ella una visión distinta; es viajero-peregrino para indagar en el alma de España para conocer capitales y aportar una nueva perspectiva. Estas tres facetas, reflejadas en sus crónicas y libros, podemos resumirlas en dos:
>
> a) Viajero eminentemente urbano.
>
> b) Viajero-peregrino, dentro de esta faceta podemos hablar de una sub-faceta; montañero-montaraz. (36)

One distinction between the two is that Unamuno's urban travels are mostly work-related,[20] and his pilgrim-traveler writings to destinations freely chosen (although, Lloréns notes, even those work-related trips constitute a form of "huidas" [38]). In his urban travels:

> Unamuno pertenece a la estirpe de viajeros que queda clasificada en lo que Pérez de Ayala llamó viaje aristocrático. Dicha estirpe no se limita a recorrer los lugares mil veces visitados por los turistas, sino que trata de aprehender ese lugar y reelaborarlo. Se trata, por tanto, de un viaje y no de un tránsito. (38)

Unamuno prepares himself well for his visits, reading local histories and the literature of native writers and conferring with residents (Llórens 37), and "Con este bagaje intelectual y humano supera a los del propio habitante de la ciudad, capta su totalidad" (38). Unamuno's urban writings, asserts Lloréns, are both "itinerario físico y guía espiritual" (38).

These writings tend to be more discursive than their counterparts, those of the "writer-pilgrim," and the Spanish section of *Por tierras de Portugal y de España* is predominantly composed of urban travel writings. In these writings, the emphasis tends to be on the factual description of the place

---

[20] Lloréns notes that: "Si atendemos a las fechas de los discursos y conferencias pronunciadas por Unamuno a lo largo de toda la geografía peninsular—fundamentalmente por capitales de provincia—y las cotejamos con los viajes que hemos dado en llamar urbanos, podemos colegir el motivo laboral de estos viajes" (36). Lloréns continues that "[t]odas las ciudades quieren recibir al personaje *público* capaz de enfrentarse a dictadores, a reyes y a repúblicas" (36) [emphasis mine], which suggests a reason for the different tone and emphasis that these writings in general have from the "pilgrim-traveler" writings.

encountered, and less on Unamuno's intimate experience of the place. A good example of this is Unamuno's extended essay "Por Galicia." Although not strictly about a city, it shares the basic properties of his urban writings. Unamuno's writings on Galicia contain some of his most sensual landscape descriptions. Galicia is a body whose geological skeleton is covered over with fleshy, feminine verdure: "Y como tal atrae a sus brazos, y llama a reclinarse en reposo en su regazo, a soñar en las haldas de sus montes" (469). However with the exception of his exclamation before the sight of a cow grazing next to the sea (a similar scene to that described in "La pesca de Espinho"), Unamuno does not include his own reactions, the thoughts and feelings that his surroundings inspire. As in *En torno al casticismo*, his emphasis is upon establishing the identity between environment and culture, this time in the region of Galicia, and not upon his own experience.

The majority of the articles on Spain in *Por tierras de Portugal y de España* is similarly discursive. Fewer exemplify what Lloréns describes as the perspective of the traveler-pilgrim. According to Llorén's:

> La preocupación constante del peregrino Unamuno es la búsqueda de su espíritu y del alma de España por sus campos y montañas. Viaja caminando lentamente en el espacio y en el tiempo al modo de los antiguos peregrinos, intentando recorrer al mismo tiempo sus paisajes del alma; se trata de una doble búsqueda. (39)

For the traveler-pilgrim, whose destination is freely chosen, "la finalidad está en el medio o el camino es un fin en sí mismo" (39). A good example of the travel-pilgrimage, however, is the piece "Excursión." (436). Unamuno states at the beginning of the article that this trip was made during his holiday in July. Again, he repeats the idea that these excursions "no son sólo un consuelo, un descanso y una enseñanza; son además, y acaso sobre todo, uno de los mejores medios de cobrar amor y apego a la tierra" (433). As Lloréns has observed, however, this search is always a "double search," and Unamuno explains that these excursions are also a vital necessity in his life:

> Y yo mismo, ¿cómo podría vivir una vida que merezca vivirse, cómo podría sentir el ritmo vital de mi pensamiento si no me escapara así que puedo de la ciudad, a correr por campos y lugares, a comer de lo que comen los pastores, a dormir en cama de pueblo o sobre la santa tierra si se tercia? A sacudir, en fin, el polvo de mi biblioteca. (439)

In this passage Unamuno also reveals his desire to present his "un-bookish" self, that is, himself as a human being more than as author, and thus he establishes parity between himself and his reader. Unamuno is not communicating the unique perceptions of a writer, but the perception of a human being who shares universal qualities with his readers.

Finally, "Excursión," like many of his more intimate pieces, has a religious element. The view from Castro de Valnera is "un paisaje musical, pero de música litúrgica, gregoriana, de pocas notas y ellas de órgano" (437). In Castañeda he visits a small Romanic church, a style of architecture he sees as particularly integrated into the landscape: "relicario de una tradición muda, que es la sal de esta tierra. Y también estas viejas colegiatas son algo de paisaje, tan de suelo como los castaños" (438). Through these associations, Unamuno imbues the landscape with religious meaning. Elements of Christian religion seem easily "naturalized," integrated into the landscape, in contrast to the aged Christ on the cross that he finds on the church's altar, "el Cristo nuestro, el Cristo berberisco, el que protesta silenciosamente contra toda europeización de escepticisimo" (438). It seems that for

Unamuno, Christianity—in his non-orthodox concept of it—is especially resonant in certain landscapes.

The two essays that follow upon this one, "De Oñati a Aitzgorri" and "San Miguel de Excelsis," which describe mountain experiences (whose meaning to Unamuno Lloréns has analyzed so well), are nonetheless essentially discursive articles. Again, I use this term to refer to those articles that emphasize informative description over the author's intimate experience. However, "Grandes y pequeñas ciudades," while not strictly a travel piece, does reveal aspects of the author's intimate experience of place. He quotes George Meredith who, writing about London, says that big cities are "the burial place of the individual man" (460). Very small towns and villages, on the other hand, present another problem: "pues falta en ella aquel mínimo de sociedad orgánica sin la cual nuestra personalidad corre tanto riesgo como puede correr en el seno de la metrópoli" (465-466). A small city, however, fosters maximum development of the individual through his frictive relation to his fellows. Relying on a determinist viewpoint (he mentions Taine) Unamuno reveals not only personal preferences, but also gives implicit advice to his readers.

In his two articles dealing with Ávila, "«La gloria de Don Ramiro»" and "Ávila de los los caballeros," Unamuno further develops his ideas on the role of one's place of residence in the development of the personality, and even the imagination, as in the case of St. Teresa: "Leyendo el libro *Las Moradas*, de Santa Teresa de Jesús, al punto se le ocurre pensar a quien haya estado en Ávila que todo ello de los castillos del alma no pudo ocurrírsele a la Santa sino al encanto de la visión de su ciudad nativa" (425). Avila is, for Unamuno, also a city to which, like the landscape in "Excursión," he attributes an essentially religious character: "tan silenciosa, tan recogida, parece una ciudad musical y sonora. En ella canta nuestra historia eterna; en ella canta nuestra nunca satisfecha hambre de eternidad" (426).

Speaking of Larreta's Don Ramiro, who perishes in Lima, home to "la poética figura de Santa Rosa de Lima, aquella santa tan genuinamente española" (419), Unamuno finds a pretext to signal the importance of the religious dimension of a nation.I quote this passage extensively because I believe it illustrates particularly well the importance of religion to Unamuno's writings on landscape:

> [E]s en el aspecto religioso donde hay que ir a buscar lo más típico y lo más radical de un pueblo. Importa poco lo que cada uno de sus habitantes, tomado en singular, piense o diga sobre religión; hay algo como un sentimiento religioso más o menos vago, y revestido de una aparente irreligiosidad a las veces, de la colectividad, y es el que mejor recoge ese sentimiento, el que mejor también representa a su pueblo. Y ni la política, ni la literatura, ni el arte tendrán eficacia y durabilidad mientras no vivan en ese sentimiento, que no hay que confundir con dogmas concretos y formulables intelectualmente. (420)

This passage is, I believe, key for understanding Unamuno's landscape writings. Landscape is for Unamuno an inspiration of and repository for religious feelings, feelings that he might find difficult to express in public language. Don Ramiro, Larreta describes, lives "con el fondo del alma" (420), a phrase that delights Unamuno as it expresses a cherished value. Part of Unamuno's intention in these landscape writings is to awaken and speak to the reader's religious sensibility, and in particular, his "hambre y sed de inmortalidad" (420). His piece on Larreta concludes with a rather negative assessment of the "professional novelist":

> No son de alabar las improvisaciones y las novelas escritas a plazo fijo [. . .]. [En] general prefiero las novelas de aquellos que han escrito pocas. Y, sobre todo, prefiero las novelas de los poetas. En

> literatura y arte no me infunden gran confianza la diferenciación del trabajo y el especialismo. (432)

As in his complaints over the exigencies of journalistic writing in "Guarda," here Unamuno again vents his conflicted attitude toward writing that is not spontaneous, not driven by some personal need outside commercial considerations or even considerations of form. However, Unamuno paradoxically makes these observations precisely from within the literary form that accounted for a significant part of his earnings. As we have seen in Azorín's writings, Unamuno also occasionally tries to disavow the conditions of his literary production from within the product itself.

Andanzas y visiones españolas

In *Andanzas* Unamuno demonstrates clear consciousness of the form that he has been elaborating in his travel writings. He expresses this awareness in his well-known prologue. Referring to *Por tierras de Portugal y de España* he says: "Constituíanlo veintiséis relatos de excursiones por ciudades y campos de la Península Ibérica y las Islas Canarias" (253), and he announces that in the present book he has collected "relatos de otras nuevas excursiones por ciudades y campos también de España" (253). He lists the various newspapers for which they were originally written (*La Nación*, in Buenos Aires, and *El Imparcial* in Spain), and explains that he has simply ordered them chronologically. Finally, he goes on to explain his motive for eliminating descriptive passages from his novels after *Paz en la Guerra*. It was to give:

> a mis novelas la mayor intensidad y el mayor carácter dramático posibles, reduciéndolas, en cuanto quepa, a diálogos y relato de

> acción y de sentimientos—en forma de monólogos esto—y ahorrando lo que en la dramaturgia se llama acotaciones. (523)

In justification of the present book, he states: "Y en cambio el que gusta del paisaje literario va a buscarlo en sí y por sí. Y a esta demanda a la afición estética es a lo que quiere responder la oferta de este libro, lector amigo" (524).

Several aspects of this prologue are noteworthy. First, Unamuno refers to a readership for literary landscapes, skyscapes, etc. Thus, Unamuno (or his publisher) has concluded that a large enough public for such writing now exists to justify the publication of this collection. I mention the impact of the publisher because Unamuno was well aware of and wrote about issues of marketing and the impact of publishers' demands on a creative product (in the epilogue to *Amor y pedagogía*, for example). In *Andanzas* itself, Unamuno somewhat bitterly remarks that his *Recuerdos de niñez y de mocedad*—which he declares to be his only published book that he intends to reread—might have had greater success had he subtitled it "ensayo de psicología de la infancia" (532). To have done this, however, would have been to "profanarlo. Nada de psicologiquerías; nada de sociologiquerías" (533). This prologue seems, more than other prologues Unamuno wrote, somewhat more geared to justifying the present book as an object of consumption than to explaining its content. Compared to other prologues, his tone here is less personal, and the prologue is also quite brief. In sum, the prologue of *Andanzas* seems too thin to be accepted as a coherent justification of Unamuno's travel writings, a form that he cultivated throughout his career (Lloréns 33).

Potentially more revealing than the prologue are his comments in "De vuelta de la cumbre," the second article of *Andanzas*. In these, Unamuno demonstrates a considerably more complex attitude to these writings than the one he shows in the prologue. At the beginning of the article Unamuno, who compares himself to a "famoso profesor de Filosofía, de cuyo nombre no quiero ahora aquí hacer mención," poses the question: "¿qué vengo a hacer?" (529). While "[l]a tarea parece fácil" (529) —write something about his recent excursion in the Gredos Mountains—in reality it is more complex: "Traigo el alma llena de la visión de las cimas de silencio y paz y de olvido, y, sin embargo, nada se me ocurre decirte de ello" (529). He goes on to say: "Algunos relatos de viajes y excursiones llevo escritos ya, pero he de dejar tal vez en el silencio en que los recojí los sentimientos más hondos que de esas escapadas a la libertad del campo he logrado" (529). For example, he has never written and does not plan to write about an experience of a sunset in Granada, when "Las lágrimas me subían a los ojos y no eran lágrimas de pesar ni de alegría; éranlo de plenitud de vida silenciosa y oculta" (530). In explanation of why he will not share these experiences, he blames his readers for their demands for a different kind of writing: "Pero ¿quién cuenta todo esto? El público, oh lector, quiere cosas concretas, noticias, datos, informaciones. Yo cada día odio más la información y me interesa menos la noticia" (530). This echoes Unamuno's statement in "Grandes y pequeñas ciudades," in *Por tierras de Portugal y de España*, that in a small city a writer "[p]uede vivir en cierta independencia de su público, sin dejarse influir por él, que es la única manera de hacerse un público en vez de hacerse uno a él" (465). While, as he notes in the prologue, there is no "más fina amistad que leerle a uno (524)," his relationship to his readership, and to these writings, is more complex. This quote furthermore reflects the tension Unamuno felt between addressing current events and describing intimate experience in these pieces that he expresses in "El sentimiento de la naturaleza" in *Por tierras de Portugal y de España.*

Unamuno follows up his stated distaste for "noticias" with an anecdote about how, during his excursion in the Gredos

Mountains, he and his companions encountered a shepherd who had only just learned of the assassination attempt on Maura several years back from an old newspaper that some hikers had left behind. The very medium for which Unamuno is writing at this moment is represented as practically irrelevant in the mountain heights: "¡Feliz mortal! Habría de estallar una revolución a sus pies sin que él se enterase" (530). Here is a paradox of Unamuno's travel writings: they are written for a medium—and would not even be possible without this medium—that is dedicated to articulating the historical moment, and in a way, to "creating" the experience of the present, of "today," and in this sense, Unamuno's writings are at odds with the mode of communication that permits them to exist. One of the unique characteristics of *Andanzas* is Unamuno's explicit address of this tension from within the form itself. This gesture parallels Unamuno's expression of his nonconformity with contemporary conditions of the novel from within the novel itself, in *Niebla*, for example (or for that matter Azorín's discrepancies with the same in *La voluntad*).

Unamuno cites Flaubert—the first volume of whose complete works happens to be awaiting him when he returns from his trip—as a kindred soul in distaste for the mundane: "¡Qué aguda, qué dolorosamente sintió la estupidez humana! ¡Cómo se dolió el burgués, el buen burgués satisfecho de sí mismo, que cada mañana, mientras toma su café con leche y su pan con manteca, se informa de las noticias de la víspera!" (531). For Unamuno, the authentic "novedad" is a sunset seen from the summit of Gredos. Furthermore, there he is free from the "preguntas, quejas, amonestaciones, reproches" (532) of, although it is not explicitly stated, his readers. Thus, in *Andanzas*, a sense of tension is evident, this time from the fact that the spaces Unamuno describes, especially the mountains, are spaces he associates with an experience of liberty, but the space of its inscription, the article, is a contested one, in which his authority is sometimes only partial.

This tension that Unamuno experiences between himself and his readership is expressed as well in his article on Salamanca in *Andanzas*. The first problem he addresses is the fact that some readers have tried to intervene in Unamuno's subject matter:

> Sí, ya sé que un publicista se debe a su público, un escritor a sus lectores, y hasta a cada uno de ellos. Pero esto tiene, como es natural, sus límites. No puede llegar a que se escriban artículos, crónicas o correspondencias criptográficas, quiero decir con clave, cuyo último sentido sólo un lector o un pequeño grupo de lectores comprenda, y tampoco se puede llegar a ponerse el escritor a merced de uno cualquiera de sus lectores que le diga: «Escriba usted sobre esto o lo otro». (628)

Unamuno says he must hold fast to this basic rule when he receives letters asking him to comment upon this or that subject "sin considerar si me interesa a mí o ha de interesar a otros lectores" (628). While Unamuno expresses thankfulness for his readers' correspondence, he is firm that his readers should not presume to "dictarme los argumentos de mis correspondencias" (628).

The second problem he addresses is that readers have also tried to indicate to him how to write about the places he chooses. His readers have complained "que me pongo en ellos; el que siempre se me ve allí; el que yo, el que unos llaman impertinente y otros satánico, se mueve y agita en las líneas todas" (629). In response, he protests that the suppression of himself in his writings does not correspond to his own vision of writing. Again, he refers to Flaubert (who appears no less than three times in *Andanzas*): "Confieso, en efecto, que no profeso las doctrinas de Flaubert respecto a la impersonalidad en el arte," which, he claims, are furthermore contradictory, and that one of the reasons he loves the French novelist's writing so much is precisely because "veo en ellas a Flaubert mismo y mucho más desde que leí su extraordinaria correspondencia privada" (629). This idea is important to understanding Unamuno's travel writings, and other of his writings as well. For example, he circumvented the proscription against the intervention of the author's voice in the novel since the solidification of realism, by staging himself (as author) as a character in *Niebla*. In addition, the prologues to his novels seem in part driven by Unamuno's insistence upon including himself in the text, and of establishing direct, "personal," author-reader communication as a fundamental part of the dynamic of reading and writing.

To summarize so far, Unamuno's travel writings can be understood as in part a reaction to the trend towards the de-personalization of writing, and as an attempt to cultivate a more intimate relationship with the reader. At the same time, he encounters resistance from readers themselves, who want to be told more "about things." It is significant that Unamuno should refer to the letters of Flaubert as his travel writings, especially many of those in *Andanzas*, often resemble epistolary writing. The tone is personal, and there is a certain consistency in the way he addresses his reader. He is furthermore free to digress from his stated subject, as one would be permitted to do in a letter. In these writings Unamuno, establishes the article as a vehicle of intimate communication between reader and writer at a moment in which prose narrative is becoming even less personal (a trend that will be canonized by Ortega). One may also recall Azorín's use of the letter format (quite infrequent in Spanish letters) in *Antonio Azorín*.

Unamuno's self-referential statements within *Andanzas* are consistent with the direction of this book toward a more intimate form of writing, and to greater inclusion of the reader. This is not to say that *Andanzas* does not contain writings as discursive as the majority of those in *Por tierras de Portugal y de España.* What occurs here is an alternation between more discursive articles and more intimate ones. The former include "Santiago de Compostela," "Junto a las Rías Bajas de Galicia," "Coimbra," "De Salamanca a Barcelona," "En la calma de Mallorca," "En la isla dorada," "La frontera lingüística," and above all "Las Hurdes," which, like Azorín's "La Andalucía trágica," is motivated by the desire to bring attention to a critical situation and to dispel prejudices. It is not that most or even all of these pieces do not contain elements of poetic evocation of place. However, the emphasis is on the places themselves and not the writer's feelings about them. (It is not insignificant that Unamuno refers to himself drawing in "Las Hurdes," as his visual artist's impulse to represent dominates here). This is not to say either that his more intimate pieces do not contain discursive elements, or even information, but what predominates is a discourse of intimate experience that he extends to the reader in an explicitly constructed relationship.

One can see the increased intimacy of tone and greater implication of the reader right from the very first piece, "Recuerdo de la Granja de Moreruela." On this trip, Unamuno contemplates "las espléndidas ruinas del primer monasterio de Cistercienses en España" (525). Unamuno explicitly separates his "interior" from his "public" voice. When his friends comment on the flora in a stagnant pond, Unamuno comments that "pensé calladamente" that it is precisely in quiet waters that flowers flourish, extending this idea to an analogy about poetry: "La industria pide agua corriente, pero a la poesía le basta la que está quieta" (525). He identifies with the ruins that long for "tiempos que se cumplieron" (526) and "me dije por adentro" a poem on the subject in which he imagines himself in a cell writing: "el poema escribir largo, muy largo" (526). Again introducing verses on the monastic life he writes: "Y yo me digo del que otra vida lleva" (527), and again before changing to his verses, “la quietud del lago del alma” (527) in which the soul immerses itself in God, “me digo” (527). Two factors are significant. Firstly, Unamuno draws attention to the fact that the voice we are hearing is an interior, intimate voice. Secondly, this voice is connected with a lyric impulse, and Unamuno’s own verses begin to invade his prose. Perhaps from *Paisajes* until now, Unamuno’s most intimate thoughts on landscape were reserved for his poetry. Now he is more explicitly attempting to integrate his lyric impulses into his prose. Finally, the tension surrounding his journalistic writing emerges again. He would like to write “largo, muy largo” (526). He follows up this thought after the verses: “¡Soñar así, lentamente, a la hora de la siesta, descansando la mirada en las charcas floridas! Y escribir un libro largo, muy largo. Un poema, y si no una historia” (526). Unamuno dreams of writings long books, but his livelihood does not often permit this process of long, slow elaboration. As a result, the intention is sketched in the brief journalistic piece that constitutes a significant part of his writers’ activity.

Finally his increasing inclusion of the reader is evident in the frequent use of the first-person plural form: “nos dice el padre Sigüenza” (526), “Oigmos de nuevo a nuestro padre Sigüenza” (527), “Y cuando andamos dentro nuestro a la busca de Dios” (527), for example. But the purpose of this inclusion is revealed most directly in the following passage:

> Sí; caminamos de espalda al sol, es nuestro cuerpo el que nos impide verlo, y apenas sabemos de él sino por nuestra propia sombra, que donde hay sombra hay luz. Detrás nuestro va nuestro Dios empuján Donos, y al morir, volvién Donos al pasado, hemos de verle la cara, que nos alumbra desde más allá de nuestro nacimiento. Esta nuestra eternidad duerme en nuestra vigilancia. (528)

The prevalence of the *nosotros* form here is marked. Unamuno is speaking not only of his own experience, but also of a condition shared with the reader. This quality is different even from the intimate writings of *Paisajes*, in which he speaks of humankind mainly in the third person, as the subject of discourse. Here Unamuno is trying to create a sense of intimate solidarity with his reader as much as to impart certain ideas. The tone is almost sermonic.

Unamuno takes up again the notion of public versus intimate voice, and the exigencies of his profession in "El silencio de la cima." Here he proposes the idea of having a period of silence:

> ¿Por qué no había de callar yo una temporada, una larga temporada? ¿Por qué no había de interrumpir mi comunicación con el público hasta que un largo, un muy largo silencio me retemplara la fibra y acaso descubrir simpatías que hoy se me escapan [. . .]. ¿Por qué este pensar escribiendo y, lo que es peor, este pensar para escribir? (537)

The anxiety over the damage to his voice by constant "public" speaking is evident, and is one principal characteristic that distinguishes *Andanzas* from *Por tierras*. But perhaps even more striking is the way that Unamuno takes this situation that is particular to him, as a highly public writer who feels conflicted with his public voice, and extends it to a universal experience that includes the reader. The transition occurs in the middle of the following passage:

> Recogerse una temporada, sí, y callar, callar envolviéndose como en mortaja de resurrección en el silencio, pero no por mezquinos móviles de defensa y de ataque, no, sino a busca de alguno de nuestros otros «yos», de alguno de aquellos que he ido dejando en las encrucijadas del camino de la vida. Pues a cada cruce de caminos que en la vida se nos presenta, cuando tenemos que

> escoger entre una u otra resolución que ha de afectar a nuestro porvenir todo, renunciamos a uno para ser otro. Llevamos cada uno varios hombres posibles, una multiplicidad de destinos, y según realizamos algo, perdemos posibilidades. (538)

In this passage Unamuno extends his own experience to universalize it and to help the reader see this moral dimension of his own life. It seems to me that Unamuno is practicing a type of discourse here that is increasingly left without a space in the literature of his time. It is the projection of a moral voice, one that could formerly have been asserted in narrative, but which is increasingly less possible due to the tendency toward suppression of the authorial voice in fiction. Unamuno is clearly interested in communicating to the reader something not only about his own existence, but also about the reader's. Here in the relatively uncodified space of the article, Unamuno achieves what is increasingly difficult in other literary forms.

In *Andanzas*, what Lloréns describes as Unamuno's traveller-pilgrim writings predominate. Within this category Lloréns has studied the subset he calls "montañera-montaraz" (36). He summarizes the importance of these writings as follows:

> la cumbre actúa como palingenesia y y al mismo tiempo es el lugar idóneo para poderse sincerar con sus lectores y consigo mismo; desde allá arriba las visiones se suceden; la fatiga—entendida como sufrimiento—y posteriormente el descanso le permite alcanzar una contemplación y una meditación apacibles —como ya sucedía en la faceta peregrina—, adecuada recompensa para el esfuerzo. (75)

One element of Lloréns' study that I wish to emphasize here is his description of the mountaintop as place where "su meditación cimera le conduce a la revelación divina" (83), in which respect he likens himself to Moses. Unamuno refers both to Moses and to the Sermon on the Mount in "Ciudad, campo, paisajes y recuerdos":

> Desde una montaña, el Sinaí, envuelta de collar continuo en fragor de tormentas, de relámpagos, fue promulgado por Moisés el Decálogo de su pueblo, y desde un monte sereno de Palestina, un olivar acaso, dulce y perfumado de sol, se vertió sobre los hombres las más santas enseñanzas. Subido en el monte [. . .] abrió Jesús la boca para dejar fluir de ella, como río que brota de una laguna montañosa inagotable, el manantial de su doctrina. (548-549)

Unamuno declares that the open air is the test of an orator: "conmover a una muchedumbre iluminada por el sol libre, dando en campo abierto, al aire libre, sus palabras" (549). These words might be self-referential, as Unamuno frequently situates himself speaking to his reader from a mountaintop. Once again, Unamuno implicitly rejects the disembodied, impersonal authorial voice. In his own travel writings, he situates himself, speaking from this or that location and acknowledging that his setting is a component of how his words transmit meaning.

In the same article, Unamuno advises that when one is in the open country, one should not read "libros en que se describa el campo mismo, libros de viajes o paisajes"; such readings are for evoking landscapes when one is at home. But if one must read, he recommends "los Evangelios de todas clases o la [lectura] de una tragedia humana" (550). That is, Unamuno suggests readings that deal with the large questions of existence, the mysteries of life and death.

Another important characteristic of Unamuno's landscapes is that they are frequently spaces of connection with one's childhood ("Al Nervión"), and to the space where one lives ("Frente a los negrillos"). As important as the determinist reading of the landscape is to Unamuno, I would argue that it is only third behind these two others. That is not to say that these are not interrelated. One of the attractions of Unamuno's writings on landscape is the way he shifts between these multiple registers. However, it is the religious dimension—or metaphysical, if one prefers, although I think the term religious is appropriate here—that gives these pieces their depth, and without acknowledging this dimension one loses much of the meaning of Unamuno's landscape writings, and especially those of *Andanzas*. The most intensely felt pieces of this collection all include some treatment of the religious experience of the spaces he describes.

His articles on Galicia—"Santiago de Compostela" and "Junto a las Rías Bajas de Galicia"—best illustrate this point. Unamuno had already dedicated an extensive article to Galicia in *Por tierras de Portugal y de España*: "Por Galicia." In this article, there is an almost conspicuous lack of religious elements in his discussion. His feminine conception of Galicia's landscape seems to resist his sense of the spiritual in landscape, which had become very identified with Castile. In his return to Galicia in "Santiago de Compostela," one almost senses a perplexity on Unamuno's part. He is attracted to Galicia—that is clear from the intense, sensual beauty of his physical descriptions—but he doesn't quite "get" Galicia, in part, I would suggest, because he has not been able to relate to this territory in a religious way. The essays in *Andanzas* are a sort of second assault on this region to which he is clearly drawn. Here, he discovers a way to relate to the region in a religious way, through the monument of Santiago's Cathedral and through the writings and biography of Rosalía de Castro. Of de Castro's writings, Unamuno singles out her poem "Santa Escolástica." In his gloss of the poem, Unamuno describes Rosalía, alone and homesick in Santiago:

> Y sólo encuentra refugio y consuelo en el templo. «Majestad de los templos, mi alma femenina—te siente, como siente las maternas

> dulzuras—las inquietudes vagas, las ternuras secretas—y el temor a lo oculto tras la inmensa altura.» Y corre la pobre aldeana al templo, se postra ante la imagen de Santa Escolástica, dobla la rodilla, inclina la frente y exclama: «¡Hay arte!... ¡Hay poesía!... Debe de haber cielo: ¡hay Dios!». (574)

The experience de Castro describes would obviously have resonance for Unamuno. Through her writing Unamuno is able to connect to the space of Santiago de Compostela through his religious sensibility, which he previously appeared unable to do. In its Christianity Galicia is ascended to synechdochal status: "El sepulcro de Santiago es el sepulcro de España toda" (575). Yet Unamuno is very conscious of pre-Christian elements of Galician culture, and wonders whether the legend of Santiago (Unamuno being skeptical about the supposed presence of his remains under the cathedral) was not a pretext to "hacer ortodoxas esas romerías con una leyenda nueva" (575).

Unamuno's ambivalence toward the Galician landscape may be rooted in his inability to connect to this space religiously, an idea that is also suggested by the article "Junto a las Rías Bajas de Galicia." Towards the end of the article—in general of the more discursive type, theorizing on various aspects of Galician culture and society—Unamuno describes coming across a little village in sight of the Ría de Marín, in which "se recogía un camposanto" (582). This little graveyard makes Unamuno and his companions—"éramos literatos ¡Dios mío! los que nos juntamos allí" (582) —think of Gray's famous elegy, as well as of a poem by Rosalía on Galician graveyards. The simple space of the graveyard is part of Christian culture, and provides a link between Unamuno's intimate self and the Galician landscape. This idea is supported by Unamuno's comments shortly thereafter on the persistence of pagan culture in Galicia: "El paganismo, que en ninguna parte murió, sino que se hizo bautizar cristianándose más o menos, late aquí más vivo que en otras regiones de España" (583). While Unamuno does not say this as a criticism (although he does seem to attribute some of Galicia's problems partly to this), it is what Unamuno perceives as the religious ambiguity of Galicia that I believe impedes his developing an intimate relationship to the landscape, except in those moments in which he can find points of religious resonance.

The particular emotion that rural cemeteries evoke in Unamuno is perhaps nowhere better expressed than in his beautiful poem "En un cementerio de lugar castellano." The clay walls of this humble cemetery make it a little island in "el mar dorado de espigas que a la brisa ondean" (758), where passing sheep seek shelter from the north wind. Unamuno empathically imagines the dead who are destined to this isolated spot, who when the rain falls "sienten en sus huesos / el reclamo de la vida" (758). The only marker of difference of this space is "la tosca cruz de piedra" that "queda como un guardián que nunca duerme , / de la campiña el sueño vigilando" (759). Only the presence of the cross mitigates the lonliness of the cemetery and its dead, and connects it to a wider sphere of meaning, as Unamuno expresses in the final verse: "¡sólo una cruz distingue tu destino/ en la desierta soledad del campo!" (759).

The religious core of Unamuno's attitude toward landscapes is also particularly clear in "Frente a los negrillos" and "La torre de Monterrey a la luz de la helada." In the former, Unamuno finds consolation in the trees whose presence accompanies him through seasons. Unamuno writes about the relationship that forms between an individual and his environment: "Si varios hombres persisten viendo mucho tiempo la misma vista, acabarán por acordar y aunar mucho de su ideación, estribándola en el espectáculo aquel. Ante un mismo árbol, toman a la postre un mismo cauce las figuraciones de los que lo contemplan" (647). In Unamuno's "horas de soledad íntima," the sight of these trees beginning to blossom again after winter "me roza quedamente, como para cerrármelas, las heridas del corazón" (648). Although Unamuno does not speak directly about religion and faith in this article, the underlying presence of these are revealed in the subsequent essay on the Torre de Monterrey. This beautiful essay on the tower within whose sight Unamuno has lived most of his adult life is very similar in subject to "Frente a los negrillos." Although the element of the environment that accompanies the author is here an architectural one, Unamuno asserts that "También la ciudad es Naturaleza; también sus calles, y sus plazas, y sus torres enhiestas de chapiteles son paisaje" (695). This is an effect of humankind's "humanizing" of nature, an idea of Unamuno's that is already present in *Paz en la guerra*.

Through this process of humanization and civilization of nature, time is collapsed into space:

> Todo es el pasado que se condensa en el presente; más que todo es la eternidad, que abarca el pasado, el presente y el futuro. Todo es el universo, y más que todo es el pensamiento. Porque el pensamiento sobrepuja a todo lo pensado y a todo lo pensable, y rebasa de ellos. (695)

This concept of concentric circles of being, radiated outwards, is mirrored by an inverse process within the contemplating individual:

> Este sueño de piedra entra al alma y cae en ella, dentro de ella, más dentro de ella: en el alma del alma, en lo que está más dentro del alma misma, y arrastra a ésta, a nuestra alma, al cimiento de las almas todas, como las olas pasajeras, al mar de las almas. (697)

It is this concept of the universe, and the position of landscape within it that allows Unamuno to conceive of the landscape as a site of permanence, where life remains in all its fullness, and also as a site of resurrection. And this concept depends on the identification of thought with the space of the universe and with God: "el reino de Dios, el reino del Hombre, es el pensamiento, qué está sobre dolor y goce, sobre odio y amor, sobre recuerdo y esperanza" (699). The tower speaks to him of the "renacimiento español, de la españidad eterna" (700), but also of the permanence of life: "me dice que la vida no es un soplo que pasa y se pierde, sino sueño que queda y se gana" (700). The meaning of landscape to Unamuno cannot be understood in without taking into account the religious sense upon which this rests.

Finally, I would like to suggest that Unamuno's decision to withdraw landscape description from his fiction might be explained not only by the reasons he states in the prologue of *Andanzas,* but also by a fundamental incompatibility between the nature of the novel and Unamuno's feelings about landscape. While multi-dimensioned, Unamuno's most intimate feelings and hopes inspired by certain landscapes are religious in character, understanding "religion" once again in Unamuno's particular conception. Not only is landscape inevitably subordinated to plot in the novel, but also the novel is historically a secular form.

San Manuel Bueno, mártir

The tension that I suggest this caused for Unamuno is resolved in a highly creative way in the novel in which Unamuno finally did return to including landscape description. In *San Manuel Bueno, mártir*, the narrador, Ángela, repeatedly identifies Manuel with the landscape: "llevaba la cabeza como nuestra Peña de Buitre lleva su cresta, y había en sus ojos toda la hondura de nuestro lago," (314) she says, and later "Ya toda ella [Valverde de Lucerna] era Don Manuel; Don Manuel con el lago y con la montaña" (315). And the lake, with its legendary town submerged beneath the surface, exerts a strong attraction on Don Manuel, who sometimes suffers a temptation to merge with it through suicide—that is, to enter the landscapes permanently, like the legendary city beneath its waters. And it is this union that Unamuno the author effects through narrative and metaphorical structure. Don Manuel is "absorbed" into Ángela's first-person account. Ángela is a maternal figure, and thus, in a way, Unamuno ennacts through this narrative structure the process of "desnacer" that he has spoken about. She is also the mediator for his figurative integration into the landscape. Ángela is herself attached to the landscape; she lacks ontic reality beyond its borders and for this reason returns to her village. Manuel's incorporation into Ángela's narrative is an intermediate step in his ultimate incorporation into the landscape. At the end of her "confessions," Ángela writes that "al escribir esto ahora, aquí, en mi vieja casa materna, a mis más de cincuenta años, cuando empiezan a blanquear con mi cabeza mis recuerdos, está nevando, nevando sobre el lago, nevando sobre la montaña, nevando sobre las memorias de mi padre, el forastero" (344). Ángela becomes part of the snowy landscape through the whiteness of her hair, but furthermore, the page she is writing becomes a metaphor for it:

> Y esta nieve borra esquinas y borra sombras, pues hasta de noche la nieve alumbra. Y yo no sé lo que es verdad y lo que es mentira, ni lo que vi ni lo que soñé —o mejor lo que soñé y lo que sólo vi—, ni lo que supe ni lo que creí. Ni sé si estoy traspasando a este papel, tan blanco como la nieve, mi consciencia que en él se ha de quedar, quedándome yo sin ella. ¿Para qué tenerla ya...? (344)

Ángela feels herself disappearing into the page she is writing; the page disappears into the snow. The narrative, Manuel within it, is figuratively incorporated into the landscape. The use of the snow is particularly effective for conveying the image of incorporation as snow is precisely something that can bury, that can incorporate the otherness of people and human objects into the landscape. Unamuno reinforces this mystical process in the conclusion of his epilogue, enunciated from "reality":

> bien sé que en lo que se cuenta en este relato no pasa nada; mas espero que sea porque en ello todo se queda, como se quedan los lagos y las montañas y las santas almas sencillas asentadas más allá de la fe y la desesperación, que en ellos, en los lagos y las montañas, fuera de la historia, en divina novela, se cobijaron. (346)

In *San Manuel Bueno, mártir*, Unamuno achieves through metaphor and narrative structure the subordination of time (narrative) to space.

It is the religious dimension of landscape that makes Unamuno's landscapes generally incompatible with the novel until he achieves a form of reconciliation in *San Manuel*. Enunciating his feelings about landscape from within the article form gives his statements greater power of referentiality than they would have within the novel. These articles point to experience beyond the text; the text supports Unamuno's desire to communicate intimate experience of a reality outside the text to the reader. The article is thus in part instrumental, not a finished and closed object of art in itself. These articles more resemble a spiritual diary and guide for the reader, to whom he extends his experience and vision of reality. In the uncodified, liminal space of the article Unamuno—whose own conflicted and unorthodox experience of religious faith would have made writing a traditional spiritual manual or treatise problematic—achieves an original, personal form of discourse with his reader.

Conclusion

Unamuno and Martínez Ruiz both made landscape a central feature of their early novels. In *Paz en la guerra*, landscape is presented through various existing modes of description that culminate in a new vision of nature as a site of intrahistoria. In *La voluntad* Azorín gives new importance to landscape description in part as a reaction against the precepts of the realist novel. In the characters of Pachico and Antonio Azorín, Unamuno and Martínez Ruiz experiment with the creation of literary doubles, embodiments of a new phenomenon in Spanish culture: the intellectual. These characters are privileged with their authors' visions of nature. Pachico articulates his experience of intrahistoria and molds his worldview in response. Antonio Azorín and Yuste converse about the importance of landscape in literature. *Paz en la guerra*, *La voluntad*, and *Antonio Azorín* share characteristics with the regional novel, and are in some respects reworkings of this genre that retain its interest in landscape and rural life, while rejecting some of the conservative ideology associated with it. In *Antonio Azorín*, Martínez Ruiz de-articulates the regional novel, ultimately reducing it back to fragments that resemble *cuadros costumbristas*, the literary form from which authors such as

Fernán Caballero and José María de Pereda previously elaborated their regional novels.

In their early memoirs, *Recuerdos de niñez y de mocedad* and *Las confesiones de un pequeño filósofo*, Unamuno and Azorín ascribe to childhood experiences of nature an important role in their artistic and intellectual development. While each memoir relates specific, autobiographical content, the authors emphasize representative and universal elements, inviting the reader's identification with their histories. For each author the experience of landscape is related to early experiences of reading and writing. The interrelationship between text and natural world that they experience will come to be an important feature of their landscape writings.

Orphanhood is an important dimension of self-representation for both Unamuno and Azorín. The attractiveness of orphan characters for these writers at least partly consists in the orphan narrative's aptness for expressing a desire for change and for a new and different future, as well as anxiety about the same. Furthermore, the orphan character is also often linked to natural spaces, which emphasize his or her solitude but at the same time present an alternative to family and social life as a source of personal identity and emotional connection. Both Azorín and Unamuno express a similar model of relatedness to landscape in their writings. By identifying them with orphans, they give their evolving literary personae a dimension of vulnerability that invites the reader's empathy and identification. This dimension of vulnerability in their public self-representation is one of the characteristics that that distinguishes them from other intellectual models. Their public voices are both authoritative and intimate. Finally, as "orphans," they also appropriate for themselves the greater freedom and potential for self-determination that is characteristic of the literary orphan.

In what are generally categorized as collections of travel writings, Unamuno and Azorín take landscape beyond the boundaries of the novel and memoir and establish it as a prose subject in its own right, in *sui generis* short writings innovated from the flexible form of the literary article. In these writings they continue their processes of literary self-creation, making use of two other forms of self-characterization: that of traveler and poet. These identities are incorporated, as well, into their continued effort to achieve a more intimate relationship with their readers. With respect to literary form, one of Azorín's innovations is his application of the urban optic of the prose poem, especially as practiced by Baudelaire, to provincial Spain. He synthesizes the prose poem and the more auctocthonous *cuadro costumbrista* to create a unique literary form, and in doing so asserts a relationship of cultural parity, not just of influence, between Spanish and French literature. Unamuno uses his travel writings to continue and extend his project of articulating national identity, to which he first gave extended expression in *En torno al casticismo*. In these writings he elaborates on the significance of Castile and also extends the scope of his essay to other regions of the Peninsula. However, the most profound dimension of his landscape writings is the religious one. This fact makes his objectives in describing landscape basically incompatible with the novel form, and may be as significant to his decision to withdraw landscape descriptions from his novels after *Paz en la guerra* as the reasons he gives in the prologue to *Andanzas y visiones españolas*.

In conclusion, in their early novels and in their travel writings, Unamuno and Azorín elaborate literary personae which reflect the changing situation of the writer in Spain. At the same time, each writer elaborated unique literary creations within the still uncodified space of the article.

Bibliography

Aguinaga Alfonso, Magdalena. *El costumbrismo de Pereda: innovaciones y técnicas narrativas*. Mesioro (La Coruña): Gráfico Galaico, 1994.

Alas, Leopoldo [Clarín]. *La Regenta*. 1884-1885. Barcelona: Bruguera, 1982.

Alvar, Manuel. Intro. *Paisajes* by Miguel de Unamuno. Madrid: Ediciones Alcalá, 1966.

Amorós, Andrés. "El prólogo de *La voluntad* (Lectura)." *Cuadernos Hispanoamericanos*, 226-227 (1968): 339-354.

Argullol, Rafael. *La atracción del abismo*. Barcelona: Destino, 1983.

Bernal Muñoz, José Luis. *Tiempo, forma y color: el arte en la literatura de Azorín*. Alicante: Universidad de Alicante, 2001.

Blanco Aguinaga, Carlos. *Juventud del 98.* Madrid: Siglo XXI, 1970.

---, *El Unamuno contemplativo.* Mexico City: El Colegio de México, 1959.

Brooks, Peter. *Reading for the Plot. Design and Intention in Narrative.* New York: Alfred A. Knopf, 1984.

Caballero, Fernán. *Clemencia.* 1852. Madrid: Cátedra, 1975.

Cardwell, Richard A. "Modernismo frente a noventa y ocho: el caso de las andanzas de Unamuno." *Anales de Literatura Española* 6 (1988).

Caseda Teresa, Jesús. "Costumbrismo y estética literaria de Fernán Caballero." *Cuadernos de investigación filológica,* T. XII-XIII, 1986-1987, pg. 69-83.

Catena, Elena. Intro. *Electra* by Benito Pérez Galdós. Madrid: Biblioteca Nueva, 1998.

Clarke, Anthony H. *Pereda, Paisajista: El sentimiento de la naturaleza en la novela español del siglo XIX.* Santander: Diputación Provincial, 1969.

Del Río, Angel and Mair José Bernadete. *El concepto contemporáneo de España: Antología de ensayos 1895-1931.* New York: Las Américas Publishing Co., 1962.

Fox, Inman. *Azorín: guía de la obra completa.* Madrid: Castalia, 1992.

---, *Ideología y política en las letras de fin de siglo* (1898). Madrid: Espasa Calpe, 1988.

---, Introduction and notes. *Antonio Azorín*. By José Martínez Ruiz. Madrid: Castalia, 1992.

---, *La invención de España*. Madrid: Cátedra, 1998.

---, Introduction and notes. *La voluntad*. By José Martínez Ruiz. Madrid: Castalia, 1989.

Franco, Dolores, ed. *España como preocupación*. Madrid: Guadarrama, 1960.

Jeschke, Hans. *La generación de 1898 en España*. Santiago de Chile: La Universidad de Chile, 1946.

Johnson, Roberta. *Crossfire: Philosophy and the Novel in Spain, 1900-1934*. Lexington, Kentucky: The University Press of Kentucky, 1993.

---, "*La gaviota* and Romantic Irony." *Cultural Interactions in the Romantic Age. Critical Essays in Comparative Literature*. Ed. Gregory Maertz. Albany: State University of New York Press, 1998.

Jongh-Rossel, Elena de. "El paisaje castellano y sus descubridores: Anticipando el 98." *Hispanic Journal*, 7 (1986): 73-80.

Jurkevich, Gayana. *In Pursuit of the Natural Sign*. Lewisburg: University of Bucknell Press, 1999.

---, "A Poetics of Time and Space: Exphrasis and the Modern Vision in Azorín and Velázquez." *MLN* 110 (1995): 285-301.

Laín Entralgo, Pedro. *La generación del noventa y ocho*. Buenos Aires: Austral, 1947.

Litvak, Lily. *El tiempo de los trenes: el paisaje español en el arte y la literatura del realismo* (1849-1918). Barcelona: Ediciones del Serbal, 1991.

---, "Ruskin y el sentimiento de la naturaleza en las obras de Unamuno." *Cuadernos de la Cátedra de Miguel de Unamuno*, 23 (1973): 211-220.

---, "Azorín's anti-Urban Philosophy." *Revista de Estudios Hispánicos*, 10 (1976): 283-296.

Lloréns García, Ramón. *Los libros de viajes de Miguel de Unamuno*. Alicante, Spain: Caja de Ahorros Provincial de Alicante, 1992.

López-Marrón, José M. *Unamuno y su camino a la "individualización."* New York: Peter Lang, 1998.

Marías, Julián. *Miguel de Unamuno*. Barcelona: Editorial Gustavo Gili, 1968.

Martínez Cachero, José María. *Las novelas de Azorín*. Madrid: Ínsula, 1960.

---, Intro. *La ruta de Don Quijote*. By Azorín. Madrid: Cátedra, 1984.

Martínez Ruiz, José (Azorín). *Antonio Azorín*. 1903. Madrid: Castalia, 1992.

---, *Las confesiones de un pequeño filósofo*. 1904. Madrid: Espasa Calpe, 1976.

---, *Diario de un enfermo. Obras escogidas*. Ed. Miguel Ángel Lozano Marco. Vol. 1. Madrid: Espasa Calpe, 1998.

---, *Los pueblos: Ensayos sobre la vida provinciana*. 1904. Madrid: Biblioteca Nueva, 1966.

---, *Los pueblos. La Andalucía trágica y otros artículos* (1904-1905). Ed. José María Valverde. Madrid: Castalia, 1982.

---, *La ruta de Don Quijote*. 1905. Madrid: Cátedra, 1984.

---, *La voluntad*. 1902. Ed. E. Inman Fox. Madrid: Castalia, 1989.

Montesinos, *José F. Pereda o la novela idilio*. Madrid: Castalia, 1969.

---, *Costumbrismo y novela. Ensayo sobre el redescubrimiento de la realidad española*. Madrid: Castalia 1960.

Pena, María del Carmen. *Pintura de paisaje e ideología: La generación del 98*. Madrid: Taurus, 1982.

Pérez Galdós, Benito. *Miau*. 1888. Barcelona: Labor, 1991.

Ramsden, H. Intro. *La ruta de Don Quijote* by Azorín. Manchester: Manchester University Press, 1966.

---, *The 1898 Movement in Spain: Towards a Reinterpretation with Special Reference to En torno al casticismo and Idearium español.* Manchester: Manchester University Press, 1974.

Rand, Marguerite. *Castilla en Azorín.* Madrid: Revista de Occidente, 1956.

Rilke, Ranier María. *Letters to a Young Poet.* New York: W.W. Norton, 1993.

Risco, Antonio. Azorín y *la ruptura con la novela tradicional.* Madrid: Alhambra 1980.

Robles, Laureano. Intro. *Nuevo mundo.* By Miguel de Unamuno. Madrid: Trotta, 1994.

Salcedo, Emilio. *Vida de Don Miguel.* Salamanca, Madrid and Barcelona: Anaya, 1964.

Sobejano, Gonzalo. "Baudelaire entre José Martínez Ruiz y Azorín." *Homenaje a Elena Catena.* Madrid: Castalia, 2001.

---, "La inspiración de Ana Ozores." *Anales Galdosianos* XXI (1986): 223-230.

---, "Ortega narrador." *Revista de Occidente* 48-49 (1985): 161-188.

Ugarte, Michael. Madrid 1900. *The Capital as Cradle of Literature and Culture.*University Park, Penn.: The Pennsylvania State University Press, 1996.

Umphrey, George W. and F. Sánchez y Escribano. Introduction, notes and vocabulary. *La Gaviota* by Fernán Caballero. Boston, New York, Chicago, Lon Don, Atlanta, Dallas and San Francisco: D.C. Heath and Company, 1930.

Unamuno, Miguel de. *En torno al casticismo*. Madrid: Alianza, 1986.

---, *Nuevo mundo*. Madrid: Trotta, 1994.

---, *Obras completas*, Vol. I. Madrid: Afrodisio Aguado, 1951.

---, *Paisajes*. Madrid: Alcalá, 1966 [?]

---, *Paz en la guerra*. Ed. Francisco Caudet. Madrid: Cátedra, 1999.

---, *Por tierras de Portugal y de España*. Buenos Aires-México: Espasa-Calpe Agentina, 1941.

---, *Recuerdos de niñez y de mocedad*. Madrid: Espasa-Calpe, 1980.

Wirth-Nesher, Hana. "The Literary Orphan as Nacional Hero: Huck and Pip." *Dickens Studies Annual: Essays on Victorian Fiction*, 15 (1986), pp. 259-273.

Valverde, José María. *Azorín*. Barcelona: Planeta, 1971.

Vidal Tibbits, Mercedes. "La dinámica de la soledad de Ana Ozores en *La Regenta*." *Actas del X Congreso de la Asociación Internacional de Hispanistas*. Barcelona: PPU, 1992.